Guaranteed Manifesting

Tibetan Buddhist Secrets for Fulfilling your Dreams

Tara Springett

Copyright © by Tara Springett, 2011
All rights reserved
ISBN-13: 978-1506162706
ISBN-10: 1506162703

Contents

Acknowledgements 4

Introduction 5

Step one - Finding the wish that brings genuine happiness 111

Step two - Harnessing the power of your unconscious mind 44

Step three - Taking action 70

Step four - Raising your vibrations 89

Step five - Overcoming craving 109

Step six - Dealing with the waiting time 128

Step seven - Removing any remaining obstacles 145

Step eight - Receiving the fulfilment of your wish 161

How manifesting really works 175

About the author 192

Acknowledgements

I wish to express my deepest gratitude to my Buddhist teachers Shenpen Hookham and Rigdzin Shikpo who taught me the essence of the Buddhist art of manifesting. Thank you to my soulmate and husband Nigel who shares and supports my journey in every respect. Without your generosity this book would not have been written. A special thank you to Gene Anger for helping me in numerous ways and for promoting this book on his website.

Introduction

When I was in my early thirties I had many wishes but most fervently I wished for a partner. Coming from a family where both my mother and my father were alcoholics and a childhood full of emotional rejection and physical and verbal abuse, I didn't exactly have a lucky start in life and from my teens onwards I struggled with a huge amount of emotional and psychological problems. But my worst problem over many years was a heart-wrenching loneliness.

But there was one ray of light in my life and that was my commitment to the Buddhist path and over the years this ray developed into a massive beam that helped me to overcome all my problems. In this process I also became a therapist and combined my psychological training with my spiritual background in order to help my clients. Buddhism is not the austere religion that some people may imagine – in actual fact:

Tibetan Buddhism embraces all desires and uses exactly this desire energy to develop us on our spiritual path and manifest our dreams simultaneously.

While most people believe that we can only do one thing at a time – namely being spiritual *or* fulfilling our desires – Tibetan Buddhism shows us a way to overcome this paradox and uses our desire energy to develop us on the spiritual path. Manifesting our dreams in this way gives us everything we want while we grow in love and compassion at the same time. The essence of the technique that I present in this book I have learnt from my Buddhist teachers. But does it work? Well, judge for yourselves – this is my story.

I wished for a partner with whom I would be happy on 'all levels' – emotionally, intellectually and spiritually. I also wanted total commitment and of course sparkling chemistry. When I talked about my dream to my many married and unmarried girlfriends they all agreed on one point - that I was being totally unrealistic. After all, I was getting on in years and surely all 'the good men' had already been taken.

Despite my friends' pessimism, I added even more details to my dream. For example, I also dreamt about a beautiful house. The house was not even so important to me – it was more like the background to my lovely relationship. In my dream it had big French windows, a white-tiled balcony and over-looked a park with a beautiful lawn and dark conifers. At the time I lived in Germany and only very few people in that country own a house. The vast majority of people live in apartments and I did not know a single person who owned a house. So – yet again - wishing for a whole house was not very realistic.

But I was still undeterred. I also imagined that the house was at a lovely lake surrounded by gentle hills, which was again something that was impossible where I lived at the time. Housing policies in

Germany do not permit houses being built around lakes because these areas are reserved for public recreation.

Another part of my dream was that I wanted to work as a Buddhist meditation teacher and self-employed psychotherapist and run sessions and meditation groups from home. Again, this was totally out of reach for me at the time: in Germany, Buddhist meditation teachings are only taught by monks or nuns and there was no chance for me to do this work. Working as a self-employed psychotherapist was not very realistic either because it would be difficult to make a living from this line of work.

So, the only 'realistic' part of my visualization was finding a partner – all my other wishes were highly unlikely to manifest. Nevertheless, guided by the teachings of my Buddhist teachers, I meditated daily on this vision for over four years.

Then one summer I went to England to take part in a meditation retreat. There I met my husband-to-be and we fell in love at first sight. It quickly became clear that it would be easier for me to join him in England as I spoke his language and he did not speak mine. So my husband-to-be set out to find us a place to live but I never told him about my fantasy of the lovely house at the lake.

When I visited my boyfriend in the following months he showed me a house that he wanted to buy for us and I got a shock - it was the house that I had visualized for years! There were the French windows and the white-tiled balcony overlooking a park with a neat lawn and dark conifers. There was even the lake with lovely hills in the distance. Everything was exactly as I had envisioned it.

My husband-to-be bought the house and we moved in. He kindly suggested that I should try to work as a self-employed psychotherapist because in England I was not qualified to work in my old line of work as a drugs counselor. Of course, I gratefully accepted. I also started to run a Buddhist meditation group because in England people accepted that a lay person can do this work. So, all my previously totally 'unrealistic' dreams had come true virtually at once.

But did it work out to be happy 'on all levels' with my husband? I can tell you after 15 years of marriage that the answer is a very joyful 'yes'.

Ever since this amazing wish fulfillment my view of 'reality' has totally changed. I have experienced in my own life that we have the ability to call into existence what we wish for even though our dreams seem to totally defy all the odds.

'Alright', you may say, 'this is a lovely story. But isn't this just another book about manifestation and positive thinking? I have already read a few and they all say roughly the same. They just don't work for me.'

This is not yet another book about positive thinking. This book is based on genuine Buddhist teachings – brought to us from a people in the Himalayas who produced more enlightened beings than most other cultures on this earth. Far too many people strive for material manifestations, only to quickly discover once accomplished, they still feel unsatisfied. If you look at the driving force behind any goal, you can easily see that all goals lead to the same destination – finding love and happiness. This book is about manifesting your dreams in such a way that you will find genuine happiness and love simultaneously.

What's more, the manifestation technique described in this book has not only worked for myself. As a therapist and Buddhist teacher, I am in the privileged position of being able to work with many people and so I see on a daily basis whether these teachings bring results. I am pleased to tell you that many of my clients and students have manifested wonderful dreams by using the exact techniques outlined in this book. And these are dreams they had not been able to manifest despite years of trying - like having a baby, a career change, a successful business, a soulmate and many more wonderful goals.

I have now worked with manifesting for over twenty-five years in my own life and I can honestly say:

There is nothing good in my life that I have not worked on beforehand with the manifestation technique outlined in this book.

I have successfully worked on manifesting my marriage, my son, my work, my health, my house, my emotional well-being, my spiritual development – and even the way I look. My unhappy childhood and early adulthood are no more than a distant memory that does not affect me emotionally at all. I am at peace with my family even though I hardly see them and am deeply happy with the life that I have created for myself.

I truly believe that we all possess a wonderful wish-fulfilling gem that we can use to make our dreams come true. If you want to know how to use your own wish-fulfilling gem, as well, read on...

Step one
Finding the wish that brings genuine happiness

Our wishes can come true and they do come true. One should actually warn people about this and tell them to be really careful about what they want because they *will* get it one day. But most people don't believe that and they carelessly wish for this and that. And when some of these wishes come true the results can be quite devastating. Let me tell you W.W. Jacob's startling story of the monkey's paw which illustrates this point quite nicely.

> *Once upon a time Mr. and Mrs. White were given a monkey's paw by an old friend. This monkey's paw, the friend said, had the ability to grant them three wishes. But he warned them and said that there was a mysterious danger involved in making these wishes and he advised the family to throw the paw away. But the Whites did not heed his advice and Mr. White wished at once for a large amount of money. Then the whole family went to bed and the next day they had almost forgotten about the mysterious monkey's paw and their wish for money.*
>
> *In the late afternoon a stranger appeared at their doorstep with a grave face. He brought Mr. and Mrs. White the dreadful news that*

their son had died at work in a terrible accident. As compensation, the stranger said, the company would give them a generous sum of money. It turned out that it was exactly the amount that father White had wished for the evening before. Mr. and Mrs. White were numb with pain and fell into a deep depression.

Ten days later Mrs. White suddenly sat up in her bed with an outcry. 'The monkey's paw', she yelled, 'we've still got two wishes!' She convinced her reluctant husband to use the paw once again to wish their son alive. And so he did.

A few hours later there was a quiet knock at the door. Their son had returned but now he had turned into a terrible monster looking for revenge. In a last effort the father used the monkey's paw for the third time and successfully wished the monster away.

This story brings home the message that we have to be very careful and wise with our wishes if we want them to make us and the people around us really happy. Manifesting the Buddhist way is the art of learning to use the power of our wish-fulfilling gem in a way that leads to *real* happiness.

The most important ingredient in finding deep happiness and fulfillment is to make our wishes with an altruistic, loving motivation.

We don't have to give up anything we want; we just need to have the motivation to contribute with our own personal desires to the well-being of others. Then and only then will we be able to create the wonderful life that we are looking for. But before we discuss the power of altruism, let's look at the basics of manifesting.

The three basic truths about manifesting

There are three basic truths about manifesting and the first truth states:

We can't be without wishes.

Wishes are at the root of everything and we wouldn't even exist without the intention to live. Even if someone is drifting through life without any big intentions, on a deep and unconscious level they still have hundreds of unrecognized desires. In other words, being alive means having wishes. This is true even if we are on a spiritual path of detachment because wanting to be detached is just another wish. The second truth of manifesting states:

We will get what we wish for.

The primordial ground of the universe *must* give us everything that we concentrate on because that is how it is designed. If you are interested in more detailed explanations about the primordial ground of the universe and why it 'must' give us what we earnestly desire you can immediately go to the last chapter of this book. If you would like to get on using your wish-fulfilling gem first, simply read on.

If we consider the first two truths of manifesting: the

inescapability of having wishes and the fact that we will get whatever we wish for (consciously or unconsciously) then it makes sense to choose our desires as wisely and as consciously as possible.

Are you aware of what you want in life? Do you know what you desire not only for your short-term future but also for your distant future and even for your future lives? Do you choose your goals in *all* areas of your life? It is important to do so because only by consciously choosing what you want can you get your hands on the steering-wheel of your life.

Exercise: Getting your hands on the steering-wheel of your life (to be done once)

Make a list of every area of your life and put them in an order so that the most important area is at the top and the least important area is at the bottom. For example: First spiritual development, second love relationships, third emotional well-being, fourth work and finances, fifth health, sixth other relationships, seventh physical appearance, eighth hobbies, travel etc.

For each of these areas write what you want.

Write a list of what you want to stop in your life.

Write a list of the things you want for the next few months, the next few years and the distant future.

Write down your wishes for the people around you.

Allowing ourselves to dream about our wishes as I

have suggested in this exercise is like taking our wish-fulfilling gem out of its precious box, admiring its beauty and feeling the tingling joy of anticipation about what it will bring to us.

There is another reason why it is so important to consciously formulate our wishes: the deep dreams we have are often like road-signs, which point to our best talents and in that way to our deepest happiness. If we do not allow ourselves to pursue our wishes we can never unfold our whole potential and we can never achieve what we were designed to achieve. In other words, our talents will be wasted and we will have to live with the frustration of an unfulfilled life.

'But aren't some wishes an escape from reality?' somebody might ask. In order to answer this question we first have to answer the difficult question, 'what is reality?'

What is reality?

Most of us believe that there is only one reality given to all of us and that we have to somehow make the best of it. But that is not true. There is not only one reality given to all of us. We all *create* our own reality. As a psychotherapist I can see every day that this statement is true. Some of my clients have *chosen* to believe that life is a misery and it is this belief that makes it very hard for them to experience more happiness. I myself have believed that as well, and I can tell you that I was 'very good' at that because I have a strong will. But then I chose to believe that there is a chance for happiness even for people with a background like mine and after some time my 'reality' changed dramatically. This world – this so-called reality – is totally different for different people according to what they believe. For one person it is hell and for another it is a paradise.

Suppose you look out of your window and see a house. At a superficial level this is simply a house. But on a deeper level we all see something different according to our deep-seated beliefs.

Someone who is paranoid may assume that terrorists are hiding in the house, ready to come out to attack. A person who is deeply depressed may think that the people in this house will never give them any kind of support and that the house is in a dismal and depressing state. Someone who feels a bit dull and uninspired may find the house boring and staid. But a person who is really happy will delight in the beauty of the very same house and in the niceness of the people living there. And for someone who is very advanced on the spiritual path this house will appear like a beautiful palace and their heart will flow over with love and compassion for the people who live inside.

So you can see that our so-called reality has as much to do with our mind as with bricks and mortar.

The interesting question, then, is what do *you* perceive when you look out of *your* window? Do you realize that you could see the same scenery in a much more inspiring way without being any less 'realistic'? The first step to experiencing our life in a much more delightful and fulfilling way is to wish for it consciously – deeply and whole-heartedly.

Choosing wishes that will make us truly happy

If we took a three-year-old girl into a huge toy shop and told her that she could have three toys of her own choice, what do you think would happen? Do you think she would wander around for a long time in order to make a wise and considerate choice? That is not very likely. It is much more likely that she would grab the first three things that looked enticing to her.

How can we make sure that we choose our wishes more wisely than a child so that they will bring us happiness? First of all, desires that are born from comparison, competition and envy will never make us happy. On the contrary, wishes like that will put us into a relentless treadmill of frustration because there will always be people who have more things than we have. In order to escape this treadmill we need to find a motivation that goes deeper than competitiveness.

Almost all wishes can make us genuinely happy if they contain one particular ingredient. Without this ingredient pursuing our aim will send us straight back on the treadmill of frustration but with this ingredient our wish, whatever it is, will turn our world gradually into a paradise. What is this ingredient?

If we want our wish to make us truly happy we need to combine it with altruistic love. This is the third truth of manifesting and it states:

Only wishes which include altruistic love can make us happy.

Combining our wishes with altruistic love means that we need to have the motivation to contribute to the well-being of *others* through the pursuit of *our own* dreams. This is the only way to find the happiness that we desire. If the unlucky White family who owned the monkey's paw had known about this simple truth they could have spared themselves a lot of misery. If they had used their paw to wish for the happiness of *everybody* they could have created happiness instead of disaster. Let me illustrate this point with another example. Imagine you want to be a world-renowned singer but you want it only for yourself and there is no love in your wish. Now think that your wish is fulfilled. You go on world tours and you sing almost every evening in full houses. At first, you love the applause you get and it gives you a real buzz. But after a few months of success you get used to all the appreciation and it fails to make you excited anymore. There is no love in your heart and at night when you go to your dark and empty hotel room you wonder why being a world famous singer leaves you so disillusioned and depressed.

How different it would be, if you added to your dream of being a successful singer the wish to use your music to make other people deeply happy. You want to touch their hearts, inspire them and take away their pain – at least for one evening. When you sing your heart flows over with love. When you hear the applause you like it but more important to you is the gratitude you feel at making people deeply happy. When you go home to your dark and empty hotel room you still carry this love in your heart and you feel like the happiest person on earth.

If our wish does not contain love and happiness for other people it will soon leave us dissatisfied. On the other hand, the more our wish is of potential benefit for all beings the more it will give us long-term happiness.

For those of you who liked maths at school I like to illustrate this point with a little diagram. (For those of you who hated maths, still have a look; it is very interesting.)

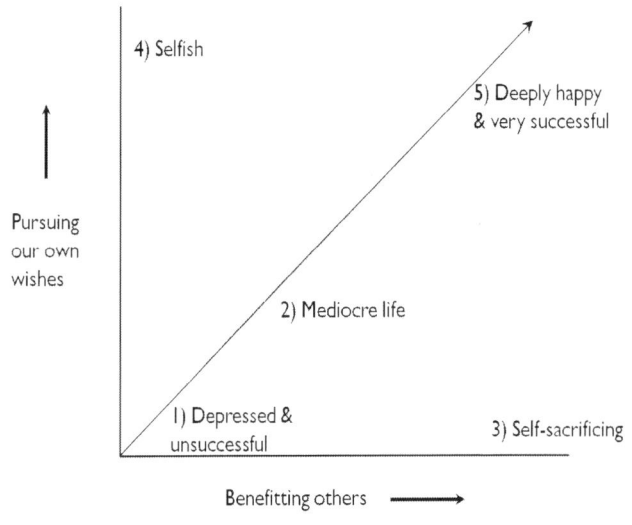

The diagram above shows:

We will be most unhappy if we don't allow ourselves to pursue any of our wishes and we don't want to make any contribution for others either. This position is one of a depressed and unsuccessful person.

If we pursue some wishes to a small degree and we have limited love for a few people around us we will get what most people have – a mediocre life.

If we think only about others and we don't allow ourselves to pursue our own dreams we can't be very happy either. An example would be a depressed and guilt-ridden mother who would rather pursue a career but who doesn't allow herself this wish.

If we think only about ourselves and we have no wish to benefit others we might get a short-lived buzz from our achievements but no deep fulfillment. I believe everybody knows at least one Mr. or Mrs. Selfish who would fall into this category.

The only place for deep happiness and fulfillment is when we pursue our own personal wishes with all our energy while at the same time wanting to help others and make them happy. Interestingly, this is also the most successful position.

Some people think that pursuing their own dreams and being full of altruistic love for others at the same time is an irreconcilable contradiction. They think that you can be either loving on the one hand or you can pursue your own dreams - but not both things at the same time. But there are always possibilities to use our own wishes to add value to the lives of others. Let me give you some examples of how people have brought these two different attitudes together:

Wanting to build up our own business *and* wanting to create excellent quality and service for our customers, earn good money for our family and create well-paid and satisfying jobs for our employees.

Wanting to have a swimming-pool in our garden *and* wanting to share it with a lot of other people.

Wanting to have a partner *and* using the love that is created in our relationship to bring more happiness to the world.

Wanting to be happy **in ourselves** *and* wanting to pass this happiness on to others.

In Tibetan Buddhism this combination of seeking our own happiness and of feeling love for others is expressed in the prayer that is repeated before every meditation:

> *May I reach enlightenment (my own happiness) for the benefit of all beings (love for others).*

The benefits of making our wishes with altruistic love

It is not 'bad' or 'wrong' to make wishes without altruistic love; it's just not very efficient – it will not bring us happiness. It can't, because the core of happiness is love and without love there will be no long-term happiness.

Before I knew about the Buddhist art of manifesting, disappointments with my wishes happened to me quite a few times because I did not possess the wisdom to pursue the right kind of desires. For instance, I wanted to have a certain job and once I got it it turned out to be the most horrible job I ever had.

Even more often, I experienced that my happiness wore off soon after because I got used to my newly reached aim. A typical example was when I earned my first money. In the beginning I was absolutely thrilled although it was only a small amount. But as time went on I got used to earning money, and eventually, the predominant emotion about my earnings was the miserable feeling that it wasn't enough. But since trying to combine my wishes with a sincere altruistic intention for others these kinds of frustrations have become far less. In the following exercise you can explore whether these Buddhist teachings are true for you, as well.

Exercise: The benefits of altruistic love (to be done once)

Think about a fervent wish that you had when you were young which has been fulfilled.

Try to remember:

How long did you feel completely thrilled about the fulfillment of your wish?

> **How long** did you feel just happy about the fulfillment of your wish?
>
> **How long** did you feel neutral about the fulfillment of your wish?
>
> **How long** did it take until you did not appreciate anymore what you had received and wanted something new instead?
>
> **If you still** feel deeply happy about the fulfillment of your wish then the chances are that your wish included altruistic love for others.

There are many more benefits of making our wishes with altruistic love and the four most important ones are outlined here:

Altruistic wishes bring us long-term happiness.

Trying to manifest our desires without having a loving attitude is like taking drugs. We might succeed and we may even be happy for a little while but sooner or later the buzz will wear off and we will be back to square one. By contrast, having an altruistic attitude is like having a guarantee that our wish will bring us long-term happiness once it is fulfilled.

Altruistic wishes make us feel more deserving.

Many obstacles in manifesting arise from deep-seated and unconscious guilt-feelings that sabotage our dream. People who were brought up in a religious way often suffer like this and can find it very hard to let this guilt go. But non-religious people often suffer from the feeling of being undeserving, too.

Combining our dreams with altruistic love solves the problem of guilt because it is in the nature of love that it makes us feel good and deserving. For example, it is easy to wish for our children to be successful, beautiful and to do well at school. Yet if we wanted all these things for ourselves we may feel a bit guilty for being so greedy. But if we felt that our own success would be good for others too, then this guilt would quickly disappear. And if we do not feel guilty anymore we can focus whole-heartedly on our wish. It is this one-pointedness that will bring results in manifesting.

Altruistic wishes come true much faster.

Wishes made with an altruistic attitude come true much faster than wishes that are only for ourselves. Just think about spiritual teachers and charities: they can attract large amounts of money for their projects without lifting a finger. Their good intentions simply attract philanthropists who are eager to help them. By comparison, someone who is out only for himself will never attract this help. This person may still become successful but it will be much harder and the success will feel somewhat hollow, like something important is still missing from their life.

This principle also applies to our own personal level. If we think of others and include them into our own wishes we will attract far more help and often experience the most unbelievable coincidences. In that way, our wishes will be fulfilled much more quickly and effortlessly.

Altruistic wishes eliminate other people's envy.

Almost every wish fulfillment can be marred or even completely destroyed by the envy coming from others. If we 'dare' to outperform our friends or family members not everyone will have a heart that is big enough to be truly happy for us. In actual fact, every great success attracts 'enemies' who either want a slice of our newly found happiness or even want to bring us down. This is not just negative thinking – if you search your memory for the times in your life when you have seriously outperformed others you will find that envy is a force to be reckoned with.

Therefore, another big advantage of altruistic love is that people won't envy you so much once your wish is fulfilled. Because they feel that they are invited to participate in your success their feelings of jealousy will often be replaced by rejoicing.

Some people may object at this point and say that all this talk about altruistic love only makes sense for saints and spiritual seekers and that it is of little value for people who struggle with mortgages and financial problems. However, these ideas are not true.

When you look at some of the most extraordinary

business success stories you will find that the principle of altruism applies to business, as well.

One example would be the gigantic success of the Internet sales company Amazon. Their success is built on one single mantra: 'customer satisfaction, customer satisfaction, customer satisfaction…..' For two whole years the company only made losses before this approach started to pay off and they embarked on one of the most impressive internet success stories. All this was achieved by putting the needs of others before their own.

I hope by now I have successfully convinced you of how important it is to develop altruistic love in general and for manifesting your dreams in particular. Now we can tackle one of the most important exercises in the whole book:

Exercise: Combine your own personal wishes with altruistic love (to be done once)

Take your list of dreams that you made earlier and add to each of your desires an altruistic wish to benefit potentially all beings. (e.g. 'I want to be a journalist in order to uncover unfairness and betrayal and to bring interesting news to a lot of people.')

Combine the things you want to stop with an attitude of altruistic love, too. (e.g. 'I want to stop having relationships with an unloving partner, so that my resources to do something good for the world are not depleted through constant arguments.')

Notice how adding a loving dimension to your

> personal wishes makes you feel more deserving and confident.

When I wished for the house at the lake that I talked about in the introduction, my altruistic intention was to run it as a Buddhist center. My husband was very inspired by this wish and he then set out to find a house that was bigger than he had initially intended. Only by adding this wish for others to the dream did he look at the house at the lake and cause my years of visualization to be manifested in every detail.

Asking your Higher Consciousness for guidance

Maybe you wonder why I go on for so long about finding your dreams. Maybe you already know what you want and all you need from this book is to be told how to realize it. However, manifesting is a powerful method and even if we are totally convinced that our wish will bring us nothing but happiness, the reality may teach us otherwise.

One way of making sure that our wishes will bring us the happiness that we want is to ask our Higher Consciousness for guidance. Our Higher Consciousness is the part of ourselves that is completely loving and wise and knows the answers to all our questions. At the same time, our Higher Consciousness is outside ourselves and we share it with all other beings. Our personal Higher Consciousness is the Higher Consciousness of the whole universe. You can perceive it in any way that feels good to you, for example, as an angelic being, as a living beautiful light or simply as one of the central figures of traditional religion.

In the following exercise I will show you a way to get in touch with your Higher Consciousness, receive guidance and at the same time start working on the fulfillment of your wish. For most of the years that I have been working with manifesting I have been using nothing else but the following exercise and it has *produ*ced miracles for me.

Exercise: The world of happiness (to be done as often as you like)

Relax and let all your tensions go with every out-breath.

You are now ready to meet your Higher Consciousness. You can see your Higher Consciousness as a shimmering light that has a living and loving quality or as a beautiful angelic being surrounded by radiant light…

See or feel your Higher Consciousness coming towards you. You can feel how your own self becomes more loving and joyful when you are touched by the beautiful presence of your Higher Consciousness…

Now ask your Higher Consciousness to guide you to find your deepest heart-wish; the wish that will truly bring happiness and satisfaction for yourself and others…

See yourself in a village in the countryside. Look around and notice what kind of houses and people you see and what the weather is like. Stroll through the streets until you reach the countryside. Notice the path you are walking on and the surrounding landscape and whether you see any people or animals...

After a while you can see in the distance a wall stretching across the whole countryside that is so high that you can't see what is happening on the other side of it.

When you come nearer you see a door in the wall with a sign that says: "The World of Happiness". This is the entrance to deep and genuine happiness. The thought of entering the world of happiness reminds you of a time in your life when you were deeply happy and for a moment you remember that situation in every detail.

Now you open the door and as you take a step into the world of happiness you immediately feel a wonderful wave of bliss welling up inside you. This feeling is full of joy and love. At the same time, it feels deeply peaceful and serene. You can see and feel how your body is filled with, and surrounded by, beautiful light.

As you look around you can see wonderful things and beloved people and you feel even more waves of happiness surging through your whole being...

You can now do anything you want. You can dance, fly and you can meet anybody you like... Don't limit

> yourself and your experience in any way. See, feel and know that your deepest wishes have come true. Everybody you encounter is as blissful and loving as you are and everybody experiences nothing else than tremendous bliss...
>
> **Stay** with these wonderful feelings and happy images for a few minutes...
>
> **Say** out loud, 'All this manifests now for the best of all beings.'
>
> **When** you are ready, come back into waking consciousness.

Don't worry if you can't 'see' a lot when you do this exercise for the first time. What counts is what you feel. Even if you can't exactly formulate your wishes after doing this practice, your positive feelings will guide you into the right direction. If you discovered new ideas about what you want in life incorporate them into your list of wishes.

Make your wish precise but not specific

To get the fastest results with manifesting we need to be precise about what we want but not specific. This means that we should not wish to buy *the specific* house at the end of *our village next week* through *this particular* real estate-agency but to wish to buy *a* beautiful house *as soon as possible* and through *the most effective and harmonious way*.

So, we should know exactly what we want but we should leave it open *when* and *how* exactly our wish fulfillment should happen. Doing this will make it much easier for the universe to give us what we want. On the other hand:

If we limit the possibilities for making our wish come true to one single outcome our wish might still come true but it will take *much* longer.

The same principle applies if we want to improve a dissatisfying situation. For example, if we work in a stressful, boring job we can wish that it will become more fulfilling. But it is much more effective to wish for *a* wonderful job without specifying whether that means that our old job improves or whether we will find a new and better job. In that way, our wish can be fulfilled in many more ways. Our old job might transform in miraculous ways but, if that doesn't happen, we might find another job that is the fulfillment of all our dreams.

Making wishes for others

Making our wishes in an unspecific way is particularly important when it comes to other people. I have received quite a few emails from people who tried to use manifesting methods to coerce another person into a romantic relationship with them. This is of course unethical and should be strictly avoided.

We can use manifesting to *invite* specific people into our life but we should never try to manipulate somebody with the manifesting method.

It is not only impossible to force our will on to somebody else in the long-term but it is also dangerous because our manipulation will come negatively back to us. If we visualize a soulmate, for instance, we can think about someone we know but we need to do that with the clear intention that this person is *just a model for our wish* and that we are not trying to impose our will on them.

If we want to make wishes for other people we can obviously support them in their aims if we know what they want. But if we don't know their goals or if we don't agree with them, we need to be very careful. From *our* point of view it might be a good idea that our son goes to law school and becomes a successful lawyer but I am pretty sure our son may have other ideas about this. The stronger we want him to do what we want, the more likely he will rebel against this. The same is true for our grumpy boss, our noisy neighbor and the friend of ours who never calls us as often as we would like.

For other people we should have only one desire - we wish them true happiness.

If somebody is truly happy they will not be grumpy anymore, they will be considerate and they will have enough energy to call us more often. Nobody will rebel against such a wish – on the contrary - people will love us for it! They will feel supported and loved and in that way they will become much happier to co-operate with us. Our son may not become a lawyer but we will definitely get a much better relationship with him.

Wishing other people to be happy is not just a nice idea. If we focus with real intent on the happiness of others it will have a tangible effect on them and change them for the better. I have seen this in my own life and with numerous clients. All of them – without exception – were able to improve their relationships by sending positive wishes to the very people who made their lives difficult. However, doing this is a topic in itself and I recommend reading my book 'The Five-Minute Miracle' for in-depth guidance.

Go beyond goody-goody wishes

Many people who work on themselves and who want to develop spiritually have a tendency to be a bit hard on themselves. One outcome of this attitude is that they often believe their desires are too selfish and they may even feel undeserving and guilty for no obvious reason. Sometimes, people think that pursuing their dreams and living life to the full is somehow 'spiritually wrong'. Unfortunately, the trouble is that this goody-goody approach often doesn't make us happy.

The more we try to suppress our 'lower' desires the more they will resurface and make our lives difficult.

For example, it is well-known that the repression of sexuality in the name of spirituality leads to neurotic symptoms. The same is true for all other forms of repression.

Tibetan Buddhism offers a wonderful solution to this dilemma. Buddhist teachers say that, from a spiritual point of view, it is not our desires that are the problem but the craving, the greed and the frustration that often accompany them. We all get frustrated if we don't get what we want. We can't help it - it's the way humans are. But suppressing our dreams is not the answer.

The best way to work with our unfulfilled greed is to *transform* it. Taking our desirous and impatient nature into account, the Buddha has given us this wonderful method of manifesting that we can use to develop spiritually *through* pursuing our personal and worldly wishes. The way to do this I have already explained: it is through combining our personal wishes with altruistic love for the potential benefit of all beings. If we work in that way every single one of our personal wishes will actually foster our spiritual development.

Another problem for people who 'work on themselves' is that they are often unable to leave a difficult situation because they believe they have to 'learn something'.

While this approach is good for many people, others go overboard and, no matter how much they suffer, they stay and try to change *themselves* in order to improve the situation. Instead of demanding that their needs are met, they are just trying to be less needy. Rather than leaving or at least rebelling against negative treatment, they are just trying to be detached and understanding. Women, in particular, tend to behave in this way.

I was like that. For many years, I never knew another way of dealing with my suffering than staying in difficult situations and 'working on myself'. But at some point, it dawned on me that there is an alternative and that I could love *myself* and change *my situation* instead. I learnt that there is no benefit whatsoever in staying in a destructive relationship if one's partner is not interested in developing more love. In such a destructive relationship we will never be able to prosper and unfold our potential. There is no benefit either in staying in a job in which our talents and qualities are not appreciated. We can try as long as we like to 'improve' ourselves - in such a situation we will never be able to be really content.

If you are a spiritual goody-goody person (like myself) and tend to go overboard with 'working on yourself' you need to be very careful that your wishes really are *your* wishes and not something you are just told to do. In order to avoid these kinds of problems you can ask yourself the following questions:

Does my wish make me tingle with joy and anticipation all over?

Do I feel positive excitement when I think of it?

Is my wish something that *I* really want in my heart of hearts?

If you can answer all these questions with a joyful 'yes' you are on the right track.

Be 'unrealistic' - go for your highest wish

Before I explain why we should be 'unrealistic' I should probably talk a little bit about the laws of attraction first. There are many misperceptions about this topic and it is important to have a clear understanding about what attracts what.

The laws of attraction

I am always surprised how often one can read that 'like attracts like' when it is so obvious that this is not true. Even as children we already knew that it is the *opposite* poles of a magnet that are attracted to each other and not the similar ones.

It is differences and opposites that create the strongest attraction in all areas of life. For example, how attracted do you feel about buying an apartment just down your road, which is more or less the same as your own? Exactly, not at all because likes do not necessarily attracts likes.

But what would you feel if, for the same amount of money, you could have a beautiful country mansion with stunning views? Or a smart city penthouse with a roof garden? Oh, that's another story – here comes a lot of attraction! Can you see, when there are differences we have attraction, when there are similarities we have less attraction.

Similarities still create a mild attraction because they provide relaxation and harmony. As an example, we might feel relaxed and harmonious in the circle of our *like*-minded friends but if a stunning person of the *opposite* sex comes along the relaxation and harmony will quickly be replaced by an excited attraction. The strongest sexual attraction always happens between two people who are most like opposites. For that reason, a very masculine man will always fancy a very feminine woman and not a woman who is as dominant and masculine as himself.

There is a third dynamic that creates attraction – we often feel powerfully drawn to what is familiar to us. This is the reason why so many people end up with the same sort of partner over and over again and why we might not try to buy a new home at all. We would rather stay in our familiar old apartment although it really doesn't suit our needs anymore.

We feel drawn to what is familiar to us because it provides us with a feeling of safety. No matter how awful the circumstances, no matter how limiting the relationships, familiarity provides security and that is a powerful glue. Although we might feel drawn to exciting new possibilities, leaping beyond our old patterns can be quite scary, as well. That is one of the most important reasons why so many people never go beyond what they have experienced in the past. Let me summarize the laws of attraction:

The strongest attraction is caused by strong differences and opposites.

We are also powerfully drawn to what is familiar to us because it provides security.

Similarities create mild attraction because they provide harmony and relaxation.

Go for your highest wish

If we want to use these insights for manifesting we need to wish for something that is really different from our current situation. We have to make a conscious choice to leave our familiar but dissatisfying patterns behind and take a courageous step into the unknown. Therefore, we should wish for resplendent health and not just for a little more energy. We should wish for a fantastic job and not just for the next promotion. We should wish to feel blissfully happy and not just 'a bit better'.

The higher our wish and the more different it is from our current situation, the more magnetic attraction it will create.

This increased attraction will *pull* us towards our desired aim rather than it being an uphill struggle. What is more, along the way all our smaller wishes will be fulfilled, as well.

If we just make small wishes we can easily get stuck. For example, if we wish for a boyfriend but we actually want a husband, we can get into serious trouble once we have our great new boyfriend and then we realize that he is not interested in marriage. It would have been much more 'economical' to wish for a husband straightaway.

'But these high wishes are not realistic!' I can almost hear the collective outcry of all my readers.

Let me repeat, by using the manifesting techniques outlined in this book we are not just trying to get the best from an existing reality – *we are creating reality*. There is no wish too high that it can't be fulfilled. Think about it, just 150 years ago much of what is normal for us today would have been totally unrealistic: curing infectious diseases, flying in the air and communicating by cell phone and over the internet, to name just a few.

All amazing scientific advances wouldn't have been possible without the passionate and fervent wishes of individuals who had only one thing in common: they had a vision and they believed in it.

We don't need to look only at scientific achievements. There also lots of smaller and bigger 'miracles' happening around us all the time, even in our own lives. There are so many stories about people who were given only a few months to live and who recovered miraculously. Maybe it even happened to someone you know. It actually happened to one of my elderly aunts who was diagnosed with cancer. Shortly afterwards, she stayed at a Christian healing center for a week. When she came back she went to her doctors and they found that the cancer had completely disappeared. The doctors were baffled but my aunt said that she had felt that 'something within her had shifted' during her spiritual retreat. We should not dismiss these events. They are important signals that there is more to this life than meets the ordinary eye. And let me ask the question again - what is reality anyway?

Most people think reality is what they perceive around them, what friends and family tell them, what scientists or priests say or what they read or see in the media. And they all think they perceive the correct view of reality.

So, how come that we all have such different opinions about what is possible and realistic? Take, for example, a colleague of yours who you dislike, a homeless person, someone rich and famous and a yogi who has meditated in a cave for the last twenty years. All these people would differ completely about what they believe is realistic in life. Why is that? We are living all in the same world, after all. The answer is that we only perceive what we *want* to perceive. In psychology this is called selective attention.

Selective attention

Selective attention means that we *cannot perceive anything other than what we believe is true*. In other words, we do not perceive reality as it is but we are constantly trying to manipulate our perception in order to confirm what we already believe. If, for example, a woman believes that all men are egotists it is very unlikely she will meet a loving man. She cannot meet him because she cannot see him. And even if she does encounter a loving man she will probably dismiss him as a bore.

Maybe all this is not new to you and you have been

familiar with these concepts for a long time. However, understanding selective attention doesn't mean being free of it. We are all complete prisoners of our beliefs about reality. The reason why most of us repeat familiar patterns over and over again is that we *can't see* that there is a better way.

What can we do about this peculiar blindness? The way out of this dilemma is *to think big*.

Thinking big

As I have already told you in the introduction, I used manifesting techniques to find a partner. I did what I ought to do and wrote a list about what I wished the man of my dreams should be like, which contained sixteen points. I also did something that I shouldn't have done and talked to my girlfriends about this list. I had a wide circle of friends then and there wasn't a single one of them who didn't tell me that I was being *completely* unrealistic. This kind of perfect Prince Charming, they told me, didn't exist or if he did, he would of course have been married to somebody wonderful for decades.

My friends didn't try to discourage me for no reason - their own reality was proof of what they were saying. They were either single themselves, divorced or they lived in mediocre or difficult relationships; they were simply trying to protect me from unnecessary disappointment.

But I kept wishing for a man with whom I could be happy on *all* levels. I am glad to tell you that I have proved all my friends wrong. Every single point on my wish-list has come true and after many years the relationship with my husband is still blossoming. So, I know from firsthand experience that it is possible to defy what most of your friends think is 'unrealistic'.

Many people are reluctant to make their wishes bigger and bolder because they feel they ought to know in advance how to make their desires come true. And because they have no idea how to do that, they don't even get started. This is a real shame because:

We *don't need to know* right from the start how to make our dream come true because by using manifesting techniques we will be *guided* to our aim.

I have seen over and over again that practicalities sort themselves out when people have a grand vision. When we use the manifesting techniques described in this book correctly, we will find the people who will help us and the resources we need in order to make our wish come true. It is really true what the old saying tells us: 'Where there is a will, there is a way'.

It is vitally important to make the altruistic part of our wish really big as well. We can wish to benefit the whole world and even future generations with our wish. The more beings we include in our wish, the greater the power that will propel us forward.

Action plan for step one

The most important action that you need to take now is:

Formulate wishes for all areas of your life so that you will not be ruled by your unconscious negative beliefs.

Combine your personal wishes with altruistic love for potentially all beings.

Make sure that your wishes really are your wishes and that they make you tingle with joy all over.

Step two
Harnessing the power of your unconscious mind

Now we will get serious! If step one was taking your wonderful wish-fulfilling gem out of its precious box, step two will explain how to use its power to work magic.

You can work on as many wishes at the same time as you like but I recommend that you choose one wish on which you want to focus primarily. This wish is called your heart-wish. If you have followed step one of manifesting, your heart-wish looks like this:

You have consulted your Higher Consciousness and you are sure that this wish comes from the depth of your being and that it is what *you* really want.

It is the highest and boldest aim you can imagine.

You have combined your wish with altruistic love so that its fulfillment will be of benefit for potentially all beings.

You have formulated your wish in an unspecific way ('*a* job in *a* great company', instead of '*this* particular job in *this* particular company').

You feel excited and joyful about your wish.

The next step is to make your wish even more precise. Why is this so important? Let's imagine the manifesting process is like ordering something from a mail-order catalogue. (In actual fact, it is so much like a mail-order catalogue that it is hard to believe).

We wouldn't just ring the friendly sales person and say 'please send me a pair of trousers'. The likelihood that they would be the wrong size, style, fabric and color is near to 100 percent. So, just as we do when we order something from a catalogue, we need to tell the universe exactly what we want. The universe will deliver precisely what we ask for, so it would be a waste of time and energy giving it vague ideas and then rejecting them afterwards.

By the way, manifesting is even better than a mail-order catalogue because it can give us so much more. From a catalogue we can order a pair of trousers with a specific size, color and cut and so on. But we can't order clothes that will definitely suit us, flatter our figure and make us feel great about ourselves. But with manifesting we can do just that.

When we 'order' our wishes we need to specify exactly how we want to feel when our wish is fulfilled. In that way we will get what is more important than anything else – the love and the happiness that we wish for.

In the following exercise you can explore in more detail how you can achieve the happiness that you wish for:

Exercise: Make your wish more precise (to be done once)

Write on a sheet of paper: 'In order to be really happy with (state here your wish), I need...

Without thinking a lot, allow a thought, a feeling or

> an image to come up and complete the sentence.
>
> **Write** down whatever comes into your mind even if it seems unrealistic or impractical.
>
> **Repeat** the beginning of this sentence a few times and each time write down what comes into your mind.

From here you can go directly to one of the most important exercises in the manifesting process. You need to write a detailed wish-list that consists of five parts: Firstly you need the description of what you want (remember the mail-order catalogue). Then you need to specify how you want to benefit others with your wish. That is the already much-discussed altruistic love-aspect. Then you need to describe precisely how you want *to feel* on all levels once your wish is fulfilled. In the next part you need to specify what you want to avoid in future.

Some self-help authors advise that any focus on what you do *not* want should be avoided because you may be unconsciously attracting it in this way. However, as a therapist working with real people I have found that the danger of being drawn into your old familiar patterns is very high, even if these familiar patterns are very painful. Therefore, it is vital to know your weak points that you tend to repeat unconsciously. The fourth part of your list will help you to become very clear what these difficult areas are and in that way help you to avoid them. Finally, write a short summary of the two or three most important and non-negotiable aspects of your wish. summary of the two or three most important and

Do not worry at this point about how your wish should be fulfilled and let the universe sort out all the practicalities. For some wishes there will be a lot of work to be done at some point. But at this point you do not need to burden yourself with all these practicalities and need simply define your wish.

Usually, it is not necessary to wish for money because it is not an end in itself. Instead, we can wish directly for anything that we would like to have and we can also wish for a feeling of financial security. There is a multitude of ways that our wish could manifest - we might even get our desired object as a gift. Similarly, don't describe *when* your wish should be fulfilled. The universe knows that you want it as soon as possible and will try to deliver it as soon as possible.

Exercise: Write a wish-list (to be done once)

Describe all the aspects of your wish.

Describe every possible detail of how you want to benefit potentially all beings with your wish.

Describe how you want to feel on all levels once your wish is fulfilled (emotionally, spiritually, mentally and physically).

Write a list of what you want to avoid under all circumstances (for example, no more destructive relationships).

Summarize your entire wish-list into the two or three

> most important and non-negotiable points.

Here are some examples of how NOT to write your wish-list:

Describe all aspects of your wish

WRONG: 'I want to be a teacher and it doesn't matter what I earn and what the school is like as long as I have a job.' (You need to be *much* more precise to find a place where you would really enjoy working.)

Describe how you want to contribute to the world with your wish

WRONG: 'I want to earn a good salary for my family'. (Ideally, your altruistic motivation would be much bigger. The bigger your altruistic wish the stronger you will be pulled towards your aim.)

WRONG: 'I just want to help the children and I don't care about the salary'. (Altruistic love does not mean being self-sacrificing. You need to wish for your own happiness, as well.)

Describe how you want to feel on all levels

WRONG: 'It isn't realistic to expect to *always* be happy'. (Are you sure? Remember, with manifesting we are *creating* reality.)

Describe what you want to avoid

WRONG: 'I don't need to avoid anything because I am such a positive and open-minded person.' (Don't be too sure. Everybody needs to make clear decisions to find a life that is really satisfying.)

And here is an example of a wish-list that has been written by a client of mine in a very skilful way:

Wish-list for a car

Describe *all aspects of your wish*: I want a safe, reliable, economical (both to buy and to run) nice looking car. It needs to be spacious – probably an estate.

Describe *how you want to contribute to the world with your wish:* My car will enable me to keep my work-commitments. It will also bring happiness to my children and friends by offering them reliable transport and by keeping my commitments to them.

Describe *how you want to feel on all levels*: Physically safe and comfortable; emotionally exhilarated and secure – also not self-conscious that I look a failure in financial (worldly) terms; spiritually that I am using the fulfillment of my wish to contribute to the increase of happiness of my students, children, friends and others.

Describe *what you want to avoid*: Owning yet another embarrassing rotten-looking rust-bucket, having oil drop on my yard, believing I only deserve the bare minimum, worrying about the vehicle, its maintenance and how I will buy my next car after this one.

Summary: Reliable, economical and decent-looking car.

My client found a car that fitted all the above points

just one week later for only half of the money he had been willing to spend.

Learning to say 'no'

Part four of the wish-list (what we want to avoid) is very important for people who have experienced the same failure in the area of their wish more than once. But some people might not like this part of the exercise because they believe that they should think entirely positively. I don't agree. One of the most important abilities for creating the life of our dreams is the ability to say 'no' when we mean 'no' and to say 'yes' only when we have found what we really want.

We are all drawn back to our past in one way or another. If our past was dissatisfying and unhappy we have to learn to say 'no' each time we are offered a repetition of our same old pattern. It is amazing how often that happens.

'No' is such an easy word – only two letters! But how difficult to say! Many of us fear losing the love and support of the people around us if we are not compliant enough and we are scared to go our way alone if nobody wants to come along.

When I was single sometimes men would fall in love with me and I received a love-letter from someone I hardly knew or some other sort of romantic approach. I tell you, that was wonderful for me. Unfortunately, from all these men approaching me there wasn't a single one who didn't have some problem with alcohol or drugs then or in their past. Even though I was not into drugs or alcohol myself, I was highly attractive for these men.

Once I attended a self-development seminary with 150 people, half of them men. At some point I got friendly with one man and we started to hug. Not much later he told me that he was a cocaine addict and that he had already spent twenty years in prison for his addiction and related crimes. At first I was shocked but then I had to laugh about his revelation. How was it possible that I could have chosen from 75 available men just the one who had such a terrible addiction?

The answer to that question is, of course, that we are always drawn to the same old patterns again and again. In order to stop meeting any more addicts I had to say 'no' many times although this really wasn't easy. Some of the men approaching me were very attractive and I really didn't like being single. If I hadn't made my strong resolution to say 'no' I am sure I would have succumbed and entered another dead end road.

Fortunately, after a while this annoying dynamic stopped and the rest of story I have already told you. The next exercise is designed to explore what exactly it is that you have to say 'no' to in order to change your life.

> ***Exercise: Learning from failures*** (to be done once and only if you had a long row of failures in the area of your wish)
>
> **Determine** the area of failures that you want to analyze (for example 'frequent relationship break-ups' or 'three times bust').
>
> **Write a** history of your failures. Write down each case of failure including how things started, how they developed and how they eventually failed. Be detailed and specific. It might be painful going through these difficult experiences but the reward of doing this exercise may be very significant.
>
> **Find out** whether all these cases had something in common.
>
> **Draw a** conclusion about what you have to change in your attitudes and behavior and where you have to say 'no' in future.

Get your whole being behind your wish

Most people think that they have only *one* personality just in the way that they have only *one* body. But nothing could be further from the truth! In each of us live a multitude of subpersonalities. On the surface we often have a goody-goody personality who only wants to eat small quantities of healthy food, say only compassionate things and work very hard.

But if we dig just a little bit deeper, we will encounter

several subpersonalities who may want very different things in life. Take, for example, the childlike subpersonality who doesn't care about working hard and eating healthy food. All *she* wants is having fun. Another subpersonality is a foulmouthed being who loves saying really nasty things about perfectly nice people.

There is nothing wrong with having many subpersonalities and it certainly does not mean that we are schizophrenic. In fact, it is natural and healthy to have many subpersonalities. Our inner genius, for instance, sometimes comes up with really original ideas.

What does all that mean for manifesting? It means that we need all our inner subpersonalities to agree on our wish. In that way, we get the power of our whole being behind our aim instead of losing time and energy by having endless fights within ourselves. What do you think the universe would do with the following message?

> *'I want to find a soulmate, but I am not sure that this is a good idea. I am too old and none of my friends have a great relationship, so it will not be very likely that I will find one, either. Maybe I should rather wish to learn to be happy on my own...but I do need somebody, I really want somebody...if only the divorce rates were a little bit lower, then I could believe that even I could succeed. Actually, I quite like to be on my own at times. And who would want me,*

anyway? I am not a beauty and I have so many idiosyncrasies; I am sure that nobody would put up with them. I want a partner but I just can't believe that anybody could really love me. I have never been really loved before and I don't see a reason why that should suddenly change.'

If we experience these kinds of unresolved inner quarrels, we will not get very far with manifesting because it is like trying to drive our car while standing on the brake at the same time.

Allowing our unconscious subpersonalities to sabotage our dream is the most important reason why so many people do not get anywhere with manifesting techniques.

Even if people visualize their dream every day, think positively and say many affirmations – if their unconscious mind is not on board they will not be successful. I see this dynamic every day in my work with clients. People think they are ready for the next step in their lives but when we take a closer look at their deep-seated beliefs, they all discover a number of obstacles that hold them back. Luckily, there is a simple way to transform most of this inner resistance.

The by far most powerful way to dissolve any unconscious resistance to our dream is to combine our dream with altruistic love for all beings.

How does an altruistic motivation dissolve our unconscious barriers? The answer is that wishing with love makes us feel very deserving. Just think of it – it is so much easier to speak up for the rights of a friend than for our own rights. There is a very deep (and usually unconscious) fear in most of us that we could be too selfish and this fear can be a big problem in manifesting our dreams. Wishing for the happiness of 'everybody' will resolve this obstacle completely. Unfortunately, there are usually more subpersonalities that sabotage our wish.

The next two exercises are designed to align all our subpersonalities behind our wish. It is very important to do these exercises because the more we become aware of how our subpersonalities sabotage our dream, the more easily we can change them.

Exercise: Find your inner saboteurs (to be done every once in a while until your wish is fulfilled)

Say out loud, 'I can make (state your wish) happen.'

Notice whether you feel that this statement is true. If you feel, 'yes, I can make my wish happen', you are on a very positive path.

If you feel, 'no, I can't make my wish happen', change your sentence to 'I do not *want* to make (state your wish) happen. Say this sentence out loud as if you mean it.

Notice whether there is a very small part of you that does not want to make your wish happen.

If you find some inner resistance that is blocking your wish, rejoice. You can be very happy that you have found an inner saboteur because now you can

> transform this 'inner enemy' into a collaborator.
>
> **Look** carefully at why your sub-personality does not want your wish to come true. This part of you may have many reasons to block your dream – some of these reasons may be reasonable and others could be outdated, negative beliefs.
>
> **Talk to** your inner saboteur and try to convince him to change his mind and join you in making your dream come true.

Doing this little exercise can be most revealing. For example, one client of mine wanted to lose weight and despite trying hard she 'just could not do it'. This is at least what she said. When she replaced 'I can't lose weight' with 'I don't want to lose weight' she discovered to her amazement that she was afraid of becoming slimmer than her sister. She feared that her sister would become envious and withdraw her emotional support. I encouraged my client to sit down with her sister and talk about her fears. Once my client had received some reassurance from her sister, she made good progress with her weight-loss.

Here is another exercise that will help you to find out whether you have some hidden saboteur that stops you from fulfilling your dream. Remember, the more inner barriers you find the more easily you can remove them.

> ***Exercise: Find out whether you have negative beliefs about your wish*** (to be done every once in a while until your wish is fulfilled)
>
> **Imagine** one morning you wake up and a miracle has happened. Your wish has been fulfilled in every detail. Obviously, you will be very happy. However, try to sense if there are any shadowy, negative feelings, as well - for instance, tiny fears or doubts.
>
> **Imagine** telling your friends and family that your wish has been fulfilled. Do you sense any shadowy negative feelings?
>
> **Imagine** living through a whole day and enjoying your fulfilled wish. Does anything negative come up – even if it is very small?
>
> **Try to** change your inner imagery so that your negative feelings disappear.

A client of mine could not imagine a happy relationship because she feared that her boyfriend could not commit. So I suggested imagining that her boyfriend would propose to her and this really alleviated her fears.

Another client could not imagine earning a good amount of money because she feared her working class family would somehow disapprove. I suggested imagining that her family would stage a party to celebrate her success. This new image helped her to overcome her inner block.

Unfortunately, sometimes our inner disagreements cannot be resolved that easily. If you find that you cannot readjust your wish in a way that takes care of all your subpersonalities try the following exercise:

> ***Exercise: Align all your subpersonalities to your wish*** (to be done once if you feel torn about your wish)
>
> **Arrange** two chairs, one for your wish and one for your sub-personality who opposes your wish. (For example, one chair for your wish for going out to work and another chair for your wish to stay at home with your children.)
>
> **Sit on** the first chair and tell your other sub-personality all about your wish and why you want it so badly. (To stay with this example, speak about all the advantages for yourself and your children of going out to work.)
>
> **Swap** seats and imagine you are the sub-personality who opposes your wish and speak about your reason, no matter how irrational and silly these reasons may be. (Tell your other part, for example, how selfish it is to want children *and* a career.)
>
> **Swap** seats again and don't get intimidated. Make your point again and try to argue against your inner saboteur.
>
> **Swap** seats several times and discuss a possible compromise. Be honest and only accept what feels like a good compromise. Such a compromise is always possible. It is in the nature of our inner subpersonalities to be able to find agreements.
>
> **Re-adjust** your wish so that your whole being with all

its subpersonalities can agree on it. You know that this is the case when you feel very good and excited about your wish.

Sometimes people have negative memories of other people who oppose their wish in some way. For example, someone who would like to find a partner may remember disappointments with their previous partner. Or someone who would like a better career remembers how their father said something disapproving about people who are too ambitious. Here is an exercise that you can use to eliminate these sorts of problems.

Exercise: Eliminate any negative feelings towards other people (to be done daily until all your negative feelings have disappeared)

Imagine yourself in a bubble of loving light, roughly as big as your outstretched hands. This bubble has a firm boundary and you feel safe and loved within it. Say to yourself with love, 'I wish myself to be happy', and feel the lovely feeling that this evokes.

Imagine an identical bubble of loving light around the other person who is causing your negative feeling. Say to them, 'I wish you to be happy' and imagine that a happy person would regret anything negative they have done and instead would help you to make your dreams come true. See the other person smiling at you and wishing you all the best.

Now let the bubble of the other person float away

> with your blessing until they have disappeared into the distance.

Create a feeling picture in your mind

Many books about manifesting say that positive thinking is the most important tool, for example, Rhonda Byrnes does so in her book 'The Secret'. Unfortunately, positive thinking is not at all enough. It is far more important to create a strong and passionate positive *feeling.* Our feelings have much more power than our thoughts and that is why we need to harness really strong emotions to make our dreams come true.

You have probably heard that it is a good idea to visualize your desired aim. However, visualizing – just like positive thinking - is not enough. We need to *feel* something as well. We need to create an emotionally charged visualization that I will call a feeling picture. Creating a feeling picture means holding an image of your wish in your mind while *feeling* love, joy and all the other wonderful feelings you wish to have once your wish is fulfilled.

In the next exercise you will learn to create a feeling picture in your mind. This feeling picture is the core of the manifesting method. By doing this you will be working real magic because it will enable you to create the miracle of calling things into existence from nowhere.

Exercise: Create a feeling picture in your mind (to be done for about five to ten minutes on a daily basis)

Relax in a way that is convenient for you.

See in your mind your Higher Consciousness in its most beautiful form and notice how you feel uplifted and loved by its presence.

Now call to mind your heart-wish and your vision about how you want to contribute to the world through its fulfillment. See everything as clearly as you can in your mind. Feel every facet of the wonderful feelings you want to feel once your wish is fulfilled. Be open to discover new aspects of your heart-wish you haven't thought of before. Stay with your feelings and inner images for five to ten minutes or longer.

Explore what kind of positive feelings your visualization evokes: what is the name of the emotion? Is it happiness, joy, peace, love or something else?

Where in your body do you feel this feeling?

If you cannot evoke strong positive feelings it is a sign that you still have a subpersonality who is not aligned to your wish. In that case, it is best to go back to the previous exercises in this chapter in order to eliminate what is holding you back.

Say out loud: '*In deepest gratitude, all this or something better comes now easily into existence for the best of all beings*'.

When you go about your daily activities try to evoke the positive feeling that is most closely related to your wish. This is your 'emotional goal-vibration'. If you wish for a baby, for instance, and the associated feeling is love, try to evoke this loving feeling even though you obviously do not have your baby yet. In other words, create *now* the emotional vibration that you wish to achieve through the fulfillment of your wish. If you wish for business success and the associated emotion is joyful excitement, try to feel this wonderful feeling as often as possible no matter what is currently going on in your life.

You have probably heard the famous saying, 'the path is the goal'. For the manifesting process this is literally true. The more we succeed in maintaining our 'emotional goal-vibration' the more quickly we will achieve our aim. It is as easy as that.

Maintaining our 'emotional goal-vibration' is often easier said than done – I know that myself only too well. It is simply not easy to feel really positive when we are missing the very thing that would make us happy. It is for this reason that there will be six more steps in this book to guide you through the process of manifesting your dream. But I want you to understand that the core of manifesting is maintaining your 'emotional goal-vibration'. I will go into more detail about the 'emotional goal-vibration' in step four.

Practice selective attention

In order to keep your mind on your 'emotional goal-vibration' it is important to practice selective attention. Instead of focusing on our failures, shortcomings and lacks you need to consciously redirect your focus on all that is positive in your life. You should also watch out for all those people who have had similar difficulties and succeeded nevertheless. If they were successful it will strengthen your confidence that you can be as well.

You also need to think about all the wishes in your life that have already come true instead of feeling bad about the ones that haven't come true (yet). If you want to have a miracle in your life, you need to read books about miracles and talk to people who have experienced miracles. The more you can fill your awareness with proof that it is possible to get what you want the stronger your faith will grow.

If you have successfully built up some faith that your wish will come true, you need to take good care that your newly found trust will not be damaged.

Don't talk to anybody about your wish who does not fully support you or who does not believe that your dream will come true.

Nothing will destroy your faith more quickly than people who think that you are unrealistic, selfish, crazy or outright stupid. Don't let this happen. Don't talk to anybody about any of your wishes unless you are very sure that they will be fully supportive. In an extreme case, that means that you will have to pursue your dream totally unsupported by the people around you. Don't let this discourage you. As time goes by, you will find more like-minded people who want the same things in life as you do and who will give you the support and inspiration you need

Create symbols of your wish

Step two seems like a lot of activity and some people might not like to do all the exercises. But believe me, when we come to letting go of craving and we are confronted with the task of non-doing, most people would be glad to do some more exercises instead of simply trying to be serene and patient.

On a deeper level, our mind is much more impressed by symbols than by words. It is for this reason that religions give us symbols and that big brands try to impress us with their logos. Once our minds have latched on to these symbols, a deep dynamic is set in motion that deepens our religious bonds or makes us buy only certain brands. For the manifesting process we can use the same mechanism by creating our own symbols so that they *pull* our deep subconscious mind towards our desired aim.

> *Exercise: Create a collage about your wish*
> (to be done once)
> **Find** pictures in magazines or on the internet that depict your wish and create a beautiful collage with them. If you are good with computers you can also do this on screen. Alternatively, you can use an

object as a symbol for your wish – for example, a ceramic house that looks exactly like the house that you would like to live in.

You can also add an occasional word to your collage to accompany your images.

As always, don't forget the part about how you want to contribute to the world with your wish.

Find a picture that shows or symbolizes your Higher Consciousness and paste it into the middle or above of your collage.

Write somewhere in your collage 'For the best of all beings'.

Look at your collage often and enjoy the prospect that everything you see will come true.

Since I have started making collages my manifesting has become much more effective. I can say that for sure because my collages have provided me with valuable feedback about how much my life has improved. Remember, I am not any more talented to make my dreams come true than anybody else. If I can do it, you can do it as well.

Make a declaration to the universe

What symbols do for our deep subconscious mind, words do for our conscious mind. On a conscious level we are more impressed by words than by symbols. Words are the missing link between our visualization and the material plane. This means that once we have formed strong ideas and images, the spoken word will give our wishes the final push into the material world.

In order to successfully use the power of our words, they need to have a certain strength and we need to speak them with confidence and conviction. We also need to make sure that everything we say will come true. If we want to strengthen the power of our word we cannot afford to break any more promises or be in any way unreliable. With every promise we keep and with every situation our words can be relied on, we will gain in power and so does our manifesting.

Another area of controlling the quality of our words is the way we talk about our problems. I personally like a good moan when things don't go the way I want because it feels so good to let off some steam. But we need to be aware that we can easily go too far into this direction. When I was younger I always complained that 'I never get what I need'. This is a good example of how *not* to talk about our problems because it creates a form of negative manifesting. I only started to get what I needed once I had completely given up saying things like that. And I only found a real soulmate after I had stopped saying negative things about men.

Words are powerful - they can hurt us more than physical pain and equally they can make us happier than many material things. Once our whole being is whole-heartedly behind our wish, as explained in this chapter, we can make a declaration to the universe.

Exercise: Make a declaration to the universe
(to be done once or as often as you like)

Plan for this declaration to be a special moment. You can create a little ceremony with candles, incense and prayer or you can go to a special place like the top of a hill.

Once your special moment has arrived, read out your wish-list and how you want to benefit others with your wish.

Then say to your Higher Consciousness and to the whole universe with conviction and authority:

'Higher Consciousness, I align myself with you as the most powerful positive force in the universe. I declare that all this or something better comes now easily into existence for the highest good of myself and all beings. I am effortlessly making every change in myself and in my environment that is necessary to reach my aim. I totally open up to receiving and enjoying all these wonderful gifts.'

Think and feel that your declaration reaches every corner of the whole universe. Know that it will connect with everybody who can help you and who will benefit from your wish and that it will draw your dream towards you.

This is what our declaration means in detail:

'Higher Consciousness, I align myself with you...' We try to become one with the most positive force in the universe in order to make our wishes as wisely and as powerfully as possible.

'*I declare...*' We *are* powerful.

'*All this or something better...*' This is a security clause in case we haven't made our wish in a completely wise way. It gives the universe the possibility of providing us with something better.

'...**comes now easily into existence**...' we don't want a lot of trouble trying to achieve our aim and we don't want to have any time delay.

'...***for the highest good of myself and all beings...***' This is our altruistic motivation which is so essential for manifesting.

'***I am effortlessly making every change in myself and in my environment...***' We and our life have to change in order to accomplish our dreams. But we want these changes to be as painless and easy as possible.

'***I totally open up to receiving and enjoying...***' It is important to be able to receive and to enjoy.

'...***all these wonderful gifts.***' No matter how powerful our declaration, ultimately our wish can only come to us as a gift and we need a humble and grateful attitude to receive it.

Let me tell you the story how Roger used a declaration to the universe to find his soulmate. Roger had been single for many years and slowly, slowly he had started to give up hope. He had had girlfriends, but nobody he wanted to marry. However, marrying was what he wanted with all his heart. One day he talked to a friend about his problem and she asked him whether he had already made his declaration to the universe. When Roger said 'no', she started to tell him off a bit and asked him how he thought he could ever expect to find his partner if he hadn't even made his declaration. Roger took her advice to heart and a few days later he went to a lonely hill top and made his declaration. Three weeks(!) later he met a lovely woman and after only a very short time he knew that he wanted to marry her.

Action plan for step two

The most important action that you need to take now is:

Write a precise wish-list of your dream

Dive into your unconscious mind and look for inner 'saboteurs'. Once you have identified unconscious resistance, let it go.

Create a feeling-picture in your mind.

Create a collage about your wish.

Make a declaration to the universe.

Step three
Taking action

Some self-help books about manifesting suggest that the inner work we have discussed in step two is all we have to do. This seems to be the case especially with the books of Esther Hicks. We simply make our declarations, think positively and then sit back and open up to receive the fulfillment of our dreams.

Unfortunately, it does not work this way – or at least not for myself or my clients. While inner work is vital – getting up and doing the things that common sense dictate is equally important. We need to study, to work, to find help and do everything possible just as we would if we had never heard anything about the law of attraction. Working with the manifesting method, unfortunately, is *not* a substitute for doing all these things. However, our inner work will make sure that all our 'outer' working will be crowned with success.

Enjoy the process

It is easy to work enthusiastically for our wish when it is new and we haven't yet experienced any major obstacles. But making wishes come true can sometimes take a long time and if we have tired ourselves out too quickly we will soon become exhausted and frustrated. And the more frustrated we are, the more difficult it is to focus on our 'emotional goal-vibration', which is so crucial.

When we work for our aim we need to do it in a

consistent way and with a positive state of mind. If you like exercise, you could think of the way you would climb a mountain as a leisure activity. It is an effort but a really enjoyable one if you do not climb too fast. It can be scary but that is part of the fun. If you hate sport, think of a creative hobby – you have to concentrate and persevere but it is so much pleasure, as well. This is the way to work during your manifesting process – with steady, enjoyable effort.

Give out what you want to get

Generally speaking, we have to put *something* out to get something back. The universe does not work on the basis that we can get something for nothing. In Buddhism, this dynamic is referred to as the law of karma. It means that we have to start a positive process by giving to other people if we want to receive.

Our giving does not have to take place only on the material level but can also be on the emotional level. If we wish to have a baby, for instance, and our 'emotional goal-vibration' is love, we should try to find ways of giving love to others. If we can do this in a consistent way, this love will come back to us - possibly in the form of a baby. Why is this so? Because the law of karma states that we will always get back what we give out.

But we can't expect that we will always get things back from the same person we gave to. On the contrary, this tactic can actually lead to the opposite of what we want. If a wife, for example, gives more and more to her husband in the silent hope that at some point he might notice and start giving something back she will often be disappointed. Instead of motivating him, her giving may actually work like a mounting debt for him, which will make him more resentful rather than grateful. Giving out what we want to get means giving in a skilful way to people who appreciate our giving so that a positive circle is set into motion.

Remember for a moment how you want to contribute to the world with your wish. It would be very beneficial if you put your altruistic motivation into practice right now. If you want to benefit a lot of people with your products and services, you may be able to start already now by supplying your friends and family with what you have to offer. If you want to be a great musician, you can start to play for people now.

This is the way many high achievers started to work in their field. They focused on what they loved to do and on how to benefit others. The appreciation, the money and the fame they finally gained grew from there as a by-product, so to speak.

Of course, there have also been plenty of rich and famous people who were less altruistic. However, one thing is sure – they certainly were much less happy and fulfilled than the more altruistic kind of people.

Whatever we want, we must not do anything that could sabotage our wish. For example, if we want to have better friendships we need to behave like a best friend ourselves. Even if others can't hear the negative things we may say behind their backs, our relentless 'karma accountant' will book everything into our accounts and one day our friends may turn against us for no apparent reason. Karma is neither punishment nor reward – it's simply the way the universe works.

Don't do it alone

Many people are fond of the idea of becoming a self-made millionaire - actually self-made billionaire these days. We like the thought that we could make it from a dish-washer to a billionaire just through our own efforts and without any outside help. But there is no such thing as a self-made billionaire. The idea is just a myth. There is no self-made successful business, there is no self-made spiritual enlightenment and no self-made successful anybody.

Everybody who achieves in their field has had help in a multitude of forms. The average millionaire/billionaire, for example, usually has a wife for emotional support and taking care of the home. Almost certainly he had supportive and intelligent business partners, funding and many more things that paved his way to success. Even people who made their first million from their bedrooms by buying and selling shares usually spend hours and hours reading the relevant literature and learning from the advice of experts.

If we want to make our dream come true, we need to seek out the help of people who are more experienced than we are.

Everybody will progress in their field of choice many times faster if they are able to recruit the help of more experienced people. It is much more effective to learn from mentors, models and teachers than through our own failures. And it hurts much less than going down the painful route of learning through emotional crisis, business bankruptcy or divorce.

When we look for people who might be able to help us it is important to communicate in a way that inspires them to work with us. How motivated would you feel to help somebody who says to you, '*I* want to be rich, *I* want to be famous and *I* want to be admired.' Probably not a lot. But what about somebody who is full of enthusiasm and outlines an idea with an emphasis on how many people would benefit from it? Somebody who has a genuine concern for others? Such a person is much more likely to attract help than someone whose exclusive interest is entirely focused on themselves.

So, at this point your altruistic motivation will once again help you to reach your dreams more easily because others are much more likely to help you if your focus is on your honest and genuine wish to help others. This approach will take many obstacles out of your way. As you can see, the idea of combining your personal wish with an altruistic motivation for others flows like a red thread through every single step of manifesting and will help you in the most amazing ways.

> ### Exercise: Speed up your progress by getting help (to be done once)
>
> **Make** a list of people who could help you to make your dream come true. This list should include people who could give you tips, people from whom you could learn by example or who could teach you and support you in any other way. On your list you could write down:
>
> **Friends** or acquaintances who have achieved what you want.
>
> **Counselors** for emotional or relationship-related issues.
>
> **Workshop**-teachers, course-leaders or any other sort of teacher you can think of.
>
> **Books**, books, books.
>
> **Biographies** of successful people from whom you can learn by example.
>
> **Self-help** groups.
>
> **Any kind** of meetings where you could meet like-minded people.
>
> **Approach** possible helpers in an appreciative and enthusiastic way and talk to them about your big vision which includes your genuine altruistic motivation.

If we look for a teacher, a mentor or a counselor we don't always need to find experts whose advice costs a lot of money. A friend or acquaintance who can do what we would like to achieve may serve the purpose just as well. When we approach someone for help it is a good idea to watch out for two criteria:

The teacher/mentor/experienced friend should make you feel good about yourself and your dreams. You will not gain a lot from a mentor relationship if it weakens your confidence even if your chosen teacher is one of the world's leading experts in their field. You would be better off with somebody who is less extraordinary but who is able to bring out the best in you through helping you to feel good about yourself, your abilities and your dreams.

The teacher should be really good themselves at what he or she is teaching. They need to have integrity and they shouldn't say one thing but then do another. To put it into the words of the old cliché, a mentor will only be of genuine help if they 'walk the talk'. So it is worthwhile to do a little bit of research before committing to someone.

The easiest way to learn and expand your skills is to find someone from whom you can learn by example. In order to do this, you need to have a little bit of humility and then simply copy from the other person as much as you can. By doing this, you will receive more than just a new set of skills. In actual fact, learning from a model will *transform* your sense of self so that you emerge as a changed person. It is this idea that lies behind the teacher-disciple relationship in Tibetan Buddhism and I think it is one of its most wonderful gifts.

When a Buddhist student has found a teacher who fits the above requirements, all they have to do is to open up in love to their teacher and the essence of this person will mysteriously be transferred to the student. It really resembles a miracle.

Everything good I have written in my books, every deeper feeling of true happiness and insight I have ever experienced comes from this slow but wonderful melting-process of my heart-mind with the heart-mind of my teachers.

Learning from a model is not limited to spiritual development. We can learn many things in that way. When I was younger I used to live in flats that I shared with different flat-mates. Years later, I recognized that I had always learnt something significant from each person I had been friends with. It always happened completely effortlessly and without me even trying. For example, I completely overcame my shyness of talking to strangers simply by travelling with a friend who was very good at it.

We don't even need to be geographically close to a person who we use as our model. All we need to do is to genuinely appreciate the positive qualities of this person and have the wish to acquire the same abilities as they have. Then we need to simply try to be and act like our model and the chances are that we will change very rapidly.

For some people, this form of receiving help is quite a challenge. They may feel as if they are losing their sense of self by copying someone else or that they are failing if they 'have to' visit a self-help group or a counselor. But the more we are able to receive graciously from positive sources, the more emotionally healthy we are and the more quickly we can make our dreams come true.

Regard your own needs as being as important as the needs of others

Now we come to the topic of finding the time to work for our aim. For many people this is a very challenging issue because time always seems too short. One of the most important guidelines to find more time is this:

To find the time to make our dreams come true we need to regard our own needs as being *as* important as those of others.

Many people in the 'self-development scene' tend to regard other people's needs as being more important than their own. Particularly, mothers find it hard to stop this self-sabotaging dynamic. For example, I have a client who is a mother of two small children. She does almost all the house work and childcare although her partner only works part-time. Another woman I know works much longer hours than her husband, organizes the entire household and childcare and doesn't object to her husband playing soccer every Saturday for the whole day. Both these women complain that they don't have the time to pursue their dreams. What can I say?

Their lives are the result of years of regarding other people's needs as being more important than their own so that there is simply insufficient energy to pursue their own dreams.

I am a mother myself and I know that it isn't always easy to pursue our own dreams when we have children. But what better model can we be for our children than to be a person who genuinely cares for others but also takes the time to make our own dreams come true? Wouldn't that be a worthwhile heritage? The same applies to all our relationships.

If we can establish equal give and take in all our important dealings with other people, we would feel so much better. Everybody values equal give and take.

Unfair relationships, where one partner is self-sacrificing and the other is selfish can only develop as an unconscious dynamic. Once both parties recognize the unfairness of the situation they will usually want to change it.

It is important to understand that it is always the more self-sacrificing partner who will have to take the lead and demand more equality. The more selfish partner who has unconsciously benefitted from the uneven situation will rarely want to change the situation on their own accord.

Being intuitive and organized at the same time

Most people I know who pride themselves on being very intuitive are pretty chaotic as well. Their houses look 'artistically' untidy and they would never even dream of writing a daily work-planner. On the other hand, most people I know who are very organized and rational don't seem to have much need to be intuitive. They get things done in a systematic and orderly way, which doesn't leave much space to listen out for intuitive ideas.

Being organized and intuitive at the same time does not need to be a contradiction. On the contrary, the less time we waste on searching for our keys the more time we have to listen to our inner voice of intuition. And the more we can put these impulses into practice in an orderly and systematic way, the quicker we will develop our field of choice.

For the more intuitive people

Let's first deal with the intuitive people who would benefit from being more organized. I will only mention two phrases, which will probably make your toe-nails cringe: 'Daily work-planner' and 'to-do list'. I am afraid nobody who wants to be successful in *this* life-time will get around them. In fact, using these two organization tools saves a lot time and takes away the guilty feeling of never really catching up with our work.

Here is an example of a really efficient to-do list: All you need is an A-list and a B-list. The A-list stands for 'urgent-list'. Here we can jot down important things like returning urgent calls or making important appointments. The B-list stands for 'All the things I can procrastinate with and still have a really good conscience' or, in short, 'procrastination-list'. Here we can jot down things and ideas that we would like to do at some point but where there is no urgency. For instance, if we want to read a certain book that has to do with our dream we can note it here because nothing terrible will happen if we put it off for a few weeks.

By dividing our to-do list into an A and B list we will be able to procrastinate only with those things that *can* be put off and actually get those things done that are really important.

The result will be that we feel much more relaxed and much better about ourselves. How do we apply all this to making our dream come true?

When we look at our dream and we think about all the things we need to do in order to make it come true, we will probably feel either rather overwhelmed or we might get into the mood of rolling up our sleeves and working like mad. In either case, it is a good idea to first sit down and write an action plan. Brainstorm and write down anything that comes to mind that needs to be done to make your wish come true. Include all problems that need to be resolved and all obstacles you need to overcome - even if you haven't the slightest idea how you should achieve that. And don't forget to add consulting all those people who could help you with your dream. In the next step, you decide on the most important things and add them to your A or B-list according to their level of urgency.

If you now feel a little bit overwhelmed, let's quickly get to the good news: Even though we do have to work to achieve our dream, we do not need to know in every detail how to achieve it and - even better - we don't need to do it all ourselves. The real beauty of the manifesting process is that, in one way or another, we will be *guided* to our dream by our Higher-Consciousness.

For the more rational and organized people

For more rational and organized people, the previous section was probably a breeze. However, they need to learn to harness their intuition so that they do not miss out on some special ideas. Our intuition is the voice of our heart and it has only one disadvantage: it doesn't speak very loudly and it isn't very assertive. As soon as we become very frenetic, too fixated on our to-do-lists and emotionally stressed, we will not be able to hear it anymore.

Sometimes it is recommended to meditate in order to encourage intuitive insight. This is certainly true but if meditation is not for you, quiet walks in the countryside or a relaxing cup of tea serve the purpose just as well. We give ourselves space, we enjoy being alive and, voila!, we have a great idea of some kind. That is intuition.

The kind of intuitive insight we receive depends largely on our heart-wish. If we want to be a healer we will receive guidance to do with healing. If we want to write a book we will receive ideas to do with our topic. And if we want to buy a house we might receive an impulse to drive around a certain neighborhood that we never thought of before. That means:

The more we know what we want (Step 1) and the more we have brought our whole being behind our wish (Step 2), the clearer the intuitive guidance we can expect.

Each step of the manifesting method is designed to enhance intuitive insight.

Combining our wish with altruistic love will connect us to our heart and the heart is the seat of intuition.

Diving into our unconscious mind and removing outdated beliefs opens the gate to our deeper mind and its intuition.

Simply asking our Higher Consciousness questions without expecting an immediate answer can be a powerful tool, as well. You may be amazed by how many of your questions will be answered if you write each of them down in a journal.

Intuitive guidance can come to us in many ways. One way is simply having a good idea. But our intuitive guidance can equally come to us in the form of a friend or even a stranger who gives us some advice, or in the form of a book cover that catches our eye as we enter a book shop or browse the Internet. It is important to follow up any of those ideas. Even if they lead to nothing in nine out of ten cases, we will be very grateful when we finally hit the nail on the head.

Intuition is wonderful but, sadly, the harder we try to be intuitive, the less it will work. Therefore, we simply need to allow ourselves plenty of space for failure without getting annoyed with ourselves. And as we become more relaxed and playful in the manifesting process, we will become happier, more intuitive and our manifesting abilities will flourish.

Behave as if you are sure that your wish will come true

This is a very enjoyable step. We need to think what we would do if we were absolutely sure that our wish will come true. Let's imagine that our heart-wish is to travel around the world for a whole year. But so far, we have never travelled more than a hundred miles from our home, we have no money and our parents would be shocked and angry if they knew what we are planning.

Working with manifesting means sticking to our wish despite all these obstacles and despite the fact that we haven't got a clue how to make our dream come true. Now we are going even one step further and *behaving* as if we are sure that our wish will definitely come true. So, we could go out and buy a small piece of travel equipment or a map of a remote area of the world. We don't need to spend an awful lot of money on these items. However, it should be enough to tell all our subpersonalities, our divine helpers and, most of all, ourselves that we are very serious about what we want.

A friend of mine is wishing for a soulmate and I suggested that he goes out and buys his (future) partner a little present and writes her a Valentine's card. Not surprisingly, he was rather reluctant. Doing things like that can be a challenge for our ego that always wants to be in charge. And the ego is absolutely right! If we start acting seriously on our wishes we begin to rely more on our Higher Consciousness, which is much more subtle than our ego that always throws a tantrum if it doesn't get its way. Relying on our Higher Consciousness means doing things that might not always make sense from an ordinary point of view. It means getting more in tune with a huge reservoir of power in ourselves that is much more loving and wise than our everyday self.

Letting go

Even more important than acquiring new things is clearing old and superfluous things out. If we want to move we should have a big clear-out to tell our subconscious that we are ready to let go of our old home. If we want better relationships we may need to let go of some of our old acquaintances.

Letting things and people go is always harder than acquiring something new. That is human – we all cling to the security of familiar people and circumstances and we often find it hard to accept that they may be detrimental to our goal. However, if we are serious about our dream we need to let go anything and anyone who is in the way of our desire. Again, we should do this by consistently regarding our own needs as being as important as those of others.

Letting go of people doesn't mean to be unloving or even to break the contact. Particularly with family members, we face the challenge of training in the high art of diplomacy. In that way, we can pursue our wishes while still relating to the people who are dear to us but who are not always supportive of our dreams.

Before I finish this section, let me say one last word of warning: Don't let other people know about your 'weird' activities involved in behaving as if you are sure that your wish will come true. They might not be supportive, which is an experience that you can happily do without.

See your activities as learning experiences

One of the biggest mistakes in manifesting is the idea that we have to do everything ourselves. What follows from this assumption is either resignation or frantic activity that leaves us exhausted and discouraged after only a short while. But if we are not very trusting and laid-back (like most people) it can be hard to give up this idea, particularly when we have worked for our wish for quite some time with no tangible results.

It can be hard to have yet another job interview when we have been rejected so many times already. It can be exhausting to go on yet another blind date if we had no luck so far. We just can't pluck up the hope that it might work this time round and, as a result, we feel exhausted and any more work feels like a terrible chore.

One way out of this dilemma is to see all our activities as learning experiences. If we go on a blind date to find a partner, for instance, we don't do it solely to find somebody but we also do it to learn about the opposite sex and the way we want to relate to others in a partnership. Through this learning experience we can adjust and refine our wishes, which is an important process. If we can see our activities of looking for a partner as a learning-process, no blind-date or dinner-party will be a waste of time because we always get something worthwhile from these events.

We need to apply the same principle to all the work we do to make our dreams come true. It is important not to let it come to the point where we feel exhausted and depressed as this will weaken our wish-power. Instead, we should try to enjoy the aspect of learning something from everything we do so that no activity will ever be a 'waste of time'.

Action plan for step three

The most important action that you need to take now is:

Give out what you want to get.

Find help.

Work for your wish in an organized and intuitive way.

Behave as if you are sure that your wish will come true.

Step four
Raising your vibrations

Imagine it was true that the universe owes us a nice life. Wouldn't that be a horrible thought? It would be absolutely maddening to think that everything that went wrong in our lives, every disappointment and every unfairness had happened *despite* the fact that the universe owes us a nice life. 'Why can it be', we would rant, 'that everybody has what I ought to have too? Why have I been left out from my fair share of the gorgeous cream-cake that everybody is munching with such smug pleasure?'

Thank goodness it isn't true that the universe owes us a nice life. How liberating to know that it doesn't owe us anything at all. We are not helpless victims at the mercy of a random and unfair God who gives to some of his children while viciously neglecting the others.

Conscious manifesting of our dreams is based on the understanding that we are the master of our destiny and with that insight comes the responsibility to seize this power.

Unfortunately, many of us lose touch with this insight and frequently revert to a sense of being a helpless victim. I don't want to blame them - I myself am often like that. I guess everybody is – another trait of being human is that we like to blame others for our own misery. However, if we want to make our big wishes come true we need to learn to act responsibly and take charge of our destiny.

Let's look at what we have done until now. In step one, we found our heart-wish and, by combining it with an altruistic motivation, we also have a guarantee that it will make us happy once it is fulfilled. In step two, we cleared out our unconscious mind of any deep-seated resistance and started to magnetize our aim by focusing on it. Then, in step three, we started to work on the outside world for the fulfillment of our wish – in both an organized and intuitive way. What else could we possibly do? Well, there is something called 'raising our vibrations' and in this step I will explain why this is so important.

Keeping our mind on our 'emotional goal-vibration'

We and our (unfulfilled) wish are not really separate because we both come from the deepest ground of the universe from which everything arises. On a deep level, we are one with everything and we can experience this in moments of our deepest fulfillment, for example when we fall in love or in the ecstatic experience of nature.

For manifesting we need to use this insight in order to avoid separating ourselves from our (unfulfilled) wish. If we *wish* to be deeply happy when we have conceived a baby but we *are* continuously depressed because we haven't conceived yet, we have a problem. By being miserable we have separated ourselves from the joy we want to feel when our wish is fulfilled. In that way, the universe doesn't have the chance to manifest our wonderful baby because our whole mind is in direct contradiction to our desire. But, as I mentioned in step two, the more we can keep our mind on our 'emotional goal-vibration' – the very feeling that we want to feel once our wish is fulfilled - the easier our dream can manifest.

Let me put it more simply: as beans grow best in rich compost, wishes grow best in a happy mind. We still need an egg and a sperm to make a baby but, ultimately, it is the state of our mind that determines the fulfillment of our deepest dreams.

From an ordinary point of view, people usually think that once their dream has manifested it will *make* them happy. However, what really happens is exactly the opposite. We need to experience a positive state of mind *first* and *then* all the wonderful things we wish for can manifest.

Keeping your mind on your 'emotional goal-vibration' means to be as happy and fulfilled *right now* as if your wish has already manifested.

Raising your vibration means improving your inner state of mind to the point where it equals the state of happiness that you are aiming for with your wish. If your mind can stabilize these wonderful feelings it will also be able to bring your corresponding wish into material existence.

Manifesting, as it is taught in Buddhism, is a spiritual path in its own right. It uses our personal desires but what it really gives us is development that goes far beyond just getting what we want. Manifesting teaches us to use our wish-fulfilling gem and, by doing so, we fall in love with it and discover that this gem in itself has everything we have always longed for.

Our wish-fulfilling gem is the essence of our mind and, by discovering its love and wisdom, we can make all our wishes come true and get in addition what no earthly desire will ever provide for us. When we experience the qualities of the true nature of our mind we will find unconditional happiness. Step four of manifesting is a first move in this direction. How can we be happy even though our wish has not yet been fulfilled?

We simply have to imagine how we would feel once our wish is fulfilled and keep focusing on this emotion as much as possible.

For some people, doing this is not difficult because they have already achieved some basic well-being. But for others it feels like trying to climb a mountain while standing on only one leg.

In order to achieve this all-important 'emotional goal-vibration' many self-help books recommend affirmations but I am not a fan of this technique. Nothing will provoke our inner resistance more quickly than the attempt to change ourselves by saying sentences that we cannot believe on a deeper level. All our subpersonalities will team up against us if we try to dominate our mind with affirmations that we are not ready for.

Raising our vibrations is easier than that. In the next few sections I will show you three ways of developing more love and happiness that really work.

Loving our wish

One of the easiest ways to raise our vibrations is to simply love our wish. If we can love our dream with all our heart, we are preparing the best conditions for it to come true. The love and the joy of our heart *are* our wish-fulfilling gem and the more we are in touch with them the easier it will be to bring what we wish for into existence.

It will not be enough if we love and admire our desired aim like an antique statue in a museum. This kind of love is too detached. In order to raise our vibrations successfully, what we need is passionate love and a lot of it!

There is a fine balance between passionate love and attachment. While passionate love is highly beneficial for manifesting - attachment is one of the biggest obstacles. Love and attachment sometimes look similar from the outside but they are complete opposites. Here is a table that explains the differences between love and attachment.

Passionate *love* for our wish	***Attachment* to our wish**
We find our desired aim wonderful and when we think of it we feel anticipation and care.	We find our desired aim wonderful and when we think of it we feel greed.
We feel a sense of well-being and genuine happiness while pursuing our aim.	We feel painful longing and frustrated desire while pursuing our aim.
We want to have our desired aim but we care for everybody who is involved, as well.	We want our desired aim so badly that we pursue it ruthlessly.
We focus on the positive contribution we want to make to the world with our dream.	We just focus on ourselves and on our desire and we don't really care if anybody else benefits from our wish.

Why is love so important for making our dreams come true? Love helps us to make our wishes come true more quickly because it is *the* most positive force in the whole universe.

In the light of love...
the body heals more quickly and pain subsides
children grow into happier and more confident

adults
difficult people mellow
plants grow more lush
conflicts are laid to rest
difficult emotions are easily overcome
our intuition improves amazingly
and wishes come true more quickly.

If we give our heart and its qualities of love, joy and wisdom more importance in our life we will improve every aspect of it. Not only will we feel much better, we will also strengthen our immune system and our relationships and we will experience much less stress. Even our intuition and intelligence will improve and we will be able to resolve all our problems much more easily. And best of all, our wishes will come true more quickly - naturally and effortlessly.

If there was an exam to be passed in manifesting, it would be the amount of love we give to our wishes and to the people we want to benefit that determines how well we achieve.

The most advanced practitioner of manifesting can virtually 'love their wishes into existence'. They feel themselves pulled towards their desire by a string that is fixed in their heart. It is the pull on their heart that will finally lead them with unwavering intuition to the fulfillment of their dream.

I wish I could claim that I am such a perfect practitioner of manifesting but I have to confess that

I am often still quite far away from this ideal. But I still seem to be able to make quite a few of my dreams come true – so you don't need to worry if you are not perfect yet, either. The universe is not so strict. Even if you do half of the required things wrong, it may still give you what you want.

I imagine that there may be some people who will say at this point, 'this is all very well for a therapist and Buddhist teacher but what about making money in a bad economic situation? Will these beautiful ideas work there, as well?' To answer this question, I would like to share the story of a good friend of mine that proves that the basic ideas of manifesting the Buddhist way works even in a hard-nosed business as real estate. This is what he told me:

> *I got my real estate license in 1989. It was a terrible market and prices had fallen over 50%. I was living in a new location, where I had no relatives, friends or even acquaintances. I noticed a lot of people tried to sell their houses themselves. I was told not to waste my time with owners who sold their house themselves as they hated real estate agents. However, I designed a complete package to help these people sell their own houses and even got 'Open House' signs with no company name made up. Then, I began approaching these people during their open houses. I offered to help them sell their own house without hiring me. I even gave them*

the signs, which I dropped off before their open house and picked up after. At the same time, I also began contacting listings which had expired from other real estate agents. Everyone in my office said I was wasting my time. After only 3 weeks of doing this, I got my first phone call, which was "come and list our house, we're fed up trying to do this on our own."

Over the next 3 months, I sold 33 houses, grossed over $110,000 in commissions, took the rest of the year off and still received the President's Gold Award from Royal le Page real estate - top 10% of agents all across Canada. All that was due to helping others. I also took the time to show other agents what I was doing and how to do it.

Wishing for others what you want for yourself

One of the most powerful ways to raise your vibration is to wish for others the same amount of happiness, love and fulfillment that you wish for yourself. If you can do that whole-heartedly, it can change your entire emotional landscape from a miserable rainy day into beautiful sunshine in a very short time.

> ***Exercise: Raise your vibration*** (to be done whenever you feel in need of raising your vibration)
>
> **Remember** the part of your wish-list that describes how you want to feel once your wish is fulfilled – your 'emotional goal-vibration'. If you wish to have a baby, for example, you probably want to feel a deep feeling of love and care.
>
> **Dwell** on these positive feelings of love until you can feel them clearly. Once you feel really good in yourself go on to the next step.
>
> **Now wish** that *everybody* in the whole world experiences the same feelings of love, as well. Of course, not everybody wants a baby but every single person in this world wants to experience this feeling of love. On this level, all human beings are totally the same. If you want success in business, wish for everybody to feel as joyful, energetic and empowered as you would like to feel. Again, on a level of feeling, everybody wants to have these kinds of emotions, no matter whether they want to have a business or not.
>
> **Make** it a habit to send out these kinds of good wishes to everyone in the world. You will be astonished how much happiness, contentment and inner calm this will bring. When your positive feelings become more stable, your wish can manifest.

The good news is that there is no shortage of happy feelings in this world - we can be totally generous with them. And the more we can send out these good wishes, the more good things will come back to us.

When a client of mine wished to buy a flat, it looked at some point as if everything in the universe had conspired against her and it started to get her down. But every time she focused her thoughts on good wishes for others she felt so much better. When the negative feelings about all the obstacles she experienced came up, she repeated several times in her mind, 'May all people have a place where they feel really at home. May all people have a home that is a peaceful haven and helps them to relax.' Saying this was enough to take away most of her frustration and to rebuild her trust that everything would work out fine in the end. Shortly afterwards she found a beautiful flat.

Making an offer to the universe

Another way to raise your vibrations is to make an offer to the universe. In order to receive your wish you need to give out in equal measure. As Napoleon Hill said in his famous bestseller 'Think and Grow Rich', we cannot get something for nothing. This insight is in line with the Buddhist teaching of karma, which states that we always get back what we give out. A very good way to incorporate these teachings into our manifesting practice is to make an offer to the universe. Doing this will have several benefits:

Focusing on giving will make you aware of how much you possess rather than how much you lack. And coming into contact with your inner richness is one of the best confidence boosters.

Making an offer to the universe will strengthen your trust that you truly deserve what we want. Deep in our unconscious mind you *know* that you can only get what you are willing to give because this is how the universe works. By making an offer you are obeying to this law and that feels deeply right.

Making an offer to the universe will bring you into contact with your inner love. It will raise your vibrations and in that way your wish can manifest much more easily

You have already formulated on your wish-list how you want to contribute to the world once your wish is fulfilled. Now you can add what you have to offer to the very people from whom you expect the fulfillment of your wish. If you wish for a soulmate, for instance, you need to write down everything that you have to offer to your future partner. This includes everything from the emotional and sexual level and everything you have to offer in the area of finances and commitment.

It is important to be honest and you should not write anything down that you don't really want to share. For example, if you don't want to marry or share your finances – you don't have to. Obviously, in that case you cannot expect a partner who would want to share everything they have, either. On the other hand, you should not hide your light under a bushel. Sometimes we have more to offer than we realize. If we want a certain job, for instance, we might not have all the required qualifications but we might be able to offer total commitment and enthusiasm.

On your list of offers you can add qualities like having a positive motivation (huge asset) and having a good heart (best asset of all). You can also include abilities like homemaking and listening skills and your *desire* to pay a good price even if you have no idea where you should take the money from at this point.

It is a scientifically proven fact that women habitually underestimate their qualities and that men do the opposite.

So, as a rule of thumb, if you are a typical woman add 25 percent of whatever you have to offer to your list and if you are a typical man look critically at your list and ask yourself if everything you have put down is really true. In either case, it can be a good idea to consult a trustworthy friend and get feedback about what you have to offer. In many cases, you will find that you have much more to give than you thought.

Once you have written your list, you need to compare it with your initial wish-list. If you see a great disparity between your two lists, you need to make some adjustments. Remember, despite the fact that we can create whatever we want, we have to obey to the law of karma as well and that means that we have to give what we want to have. If you are a sixty year old man and you want to have a gorgeous twenty-year old girlfriend, you will have a problem. Or if you want to be a great musician but you don't offer time, discipline and dedication to learn your instrument something is wrong, as well.

On the other hand, if you are a capable woman but you don't dare to apply for the best career positions or you do not demand equality in your relationship, you are not appreciating yourself enough. When you focus on what you have to give you need to fully value yourself.

> *Exercise: Make an offer to the universe* (to be done once)
>
> **Write** a list of everything that you have to offer in the area of your wish. Include not only your abilities, your finances but also your attitudes, your emotions and your intentions. Compare this list with your initial wish-list and decide if your offer matches your desire. If it does, great – if it doesn't, try to adjust your offer or your wish until you get roughly an even match.
>
> **Plan for** a special time and place to make your offer to the universe. If you like, you can include some incense, ritual and prayer.
>
> **When** the time has arrived, read out your offer to the universe with passion and dedication. Then add '*I invite all people who like my offer to come to me now for the best of all beings.*'
>
> **Keep** the list of your offer in a special place and read it through from time to time.
>
> **Frequently** dwell on what you have to offer to others – particularly when you feel under-confident.

For many people it feels deeply empowering to send

out not only wishes but offers as well. Think about anybody who is very successful and genuinely happy. No matter in what field these people excel, they usually have one thing in common: they all have a lot to offer to other people.

The ultimate way of raising our vibrations

I will now reveal to you what I consider the ultimate way of raising our vibrations and manifesting what you want to achieve at the highest speed. The following exercise is derived from the meditation that is at the heart of Tibetan Buddhism and it has produced amazing results for many people.

This exercise uses the power contained in the different energy centers of our body – our chakras. According to Tibetan Buddhism, there are five main chakras located in the forehead, throat, chest, solar plexus (upper abdomen) and navel (lower abdomen). Within our chakras we hold all our beliefs and associated emotions about ourselves, other people and life in general.

According to Tibetan Buddhism, our reality emerges from the state of our chakras in the same way that images emerge from an old-fashioned film projector. The images on the film roll are equivalent to our wishes and attitudes. The light that projects the images on to the cinema screen represents our desire and emotional intensity. The stronger our desire/light the brighter the images will be. And the images on the screen are the 'reality' that surrounds us and produces the different 'worlds' that we live in.

So, the most important thing for changing our reality is to change the state of our chakras and clear out any negative ideas and emotions.

Chakra change equals life change

Just like a speck of dust on a film roll appears as a big stain on a cinema screen, so even a small negative attitude in our chakras will appear magnified as the 'reality' that surrounds us. It is for this reason that we need to purify our chakras through changing our attitudes and emotions in order to experience the life of our dreams.

It is important to understand that all five chakras need to work in harmony. Any discrepancy between our five different chakras will result in disturbing and confusing experiences.

For example, with our head chakra we may envisage ourselves as a charismatic teacher but a block in our throat chakra may make us stutter and thus destroy this dream. Another very common discrepancy is between the navel and the heart. Many of my clients who are looking for a soulmate experience this problem. It consists of being drawn to one kind of person from the heart but sexually being drawn to someone completely different. It seems as if love and sex are incompatible and creates either sexually exciting but emotionally dissatisfying relationships or loving relationships without the right amount of chemistry.

So, the challenge we face is to purify our mind of all its negative attitudes and — even more importantly — get all our chakras in total harmony to form *one positive image* that can then manifest as our tangible reality. To use the example of a soulmate again - we need to get our navel (sex) and heart chakra (love) into complete harmony in order to find a partner who is loving *and* sexy.

Whenever we have a hard time manifesting our dream we can be sure that there is at least one chakra that is out of alignment with the other chakras and sabotages all our efforts. We already touched on this topic when we discussed our various subpersonalities that may sabotage our dreams. Talking about chakras is just another way of describing this problem. The exercise below will help you to identify which chakra is creating the problem and bring it back on track with the others.

Location of the chakras

There is no need to worry about the exact location of each chakra as they are not material things but states of mind that manifest in different areas of the body. Accordingly, the location of the chakras slightly varies from person to person. It is enough if you broadly focus into the centre of your forehead, throat or chest and simply notice where you feel most positive feelings.

The solar plexus chakra is located just below the rib

cage in the area of your physical stomach and the navel chakra is located directly behind your navel or slightly below and it extends right down to the genitals.

The following exercise is the most condensed form of manifesting and therefore the most important. If you want to practice only one exercise you should first write your wish-list and then practice daily the following meditation.

> ***Exercise: Chakra practice to manifest your dreams**** (to be done daily until your wish has manifested)
>
> **Visualize** that your wish is fulfilled and benefits others in the process. Feel the positive feeling that these inner images evoke.
>
> **Identify** where in your body you feel the most intense positive feeling (for example, in your heart or stomach).
>
> **Imagine** a beam of light full of these happy feelings going out from this part of your body towards the people involved in your aim and entering the same place in their bodies (for example, a beam of light between your and their hearts).
>
> **Feel** happy, loving energy coming back from these people to you and feel the beam of light entering into your own chakra. This process should feel intensely enjoyable.
>
> **Feel** energy going back and forth between your chakra and the corresponding chakra of the people

involved in your wish and deeply enjoy that feeling.

Go to another chakra (e.g. head, throat, heart, solar plexus and navel) and imagine great happiness in this chakra too until you can feel it clearly. Create another beam of light from this chakra full of happy feelings going back and forth between you and the other people involved in your wish.

Go through all five chakras – one at a time – and create similar beams of light.

Notice which chakra feels numb or filled with pain or negative emotions. Be pleased that you have identified a block because you can now start to remove it using the following technique: Start with deeply relaxing this part of your body.

Then imagine a tight flower bud in the area of the pain or numbness. Visualize sending love and happiness to this flower bud enveloping it with loving light. With each out breath see this flower bud opening up blossoming into a beautiful bright flower. Patiently relax the chakra in this way until you can experience a happy feeling in this area of your body. Once you can feel the positive emotion create the beam of light sending love and happiness.

Finally, try to hold all five beams of light and happiness simultaneously and strongly feel that you and your wish have become one.

This exercise is the ultimate exercise to call into existence anything you desire and you should practice it daily until your wish has manifested. Focus equally on energy going out from you (giving) and coming back into you (receiving). If possible, try to feel the happy feelings of all five beams simultaneously. Do not be concerned if this is difficult in the beginning. If it was easy you would not be reading this book but would already be enjoying the fulfillment of your wish. Chakra change means life change!

Action plan for step four

The most important actions that you need to take now are:

Keep your mind on your 'emotional goal-vibration' as much as you can.

Wish for others to feel in the way that you want to feel yourself.

Make an offer to the universe.

Practice the chakra meditation every day – it is the most important exercise in this book.

Step five
Overcoming craving

In Steps one to four of manifesting we have basically learnt everything we need to do in order to make our wishes come true: Finding our heart-wish, using the power of our mind, working efficiently for our wish and raising our vibrations. That's all!

The next four steps will focus on everything we *shouldn't* do that would mess up the beautiful process of letting things arise from the primordial ground of the universe. There are so many pitfalls and traps we can encounter that they deserve four more steps so that we can successfully avoid them.

The greatest 'evil' in manifesting is craving and attachment. Craving is basically every bad feeling around our wish: greed, painful longing, impatience, frustration, anger, worrying, hopelessness, depression, despair, obsessive thinking and so on.

Whenever we have a wish and we grow impatient and develop one of these negative feelings, we are at risk of spoiling the process of manifesting. This is a pretty big risk, I admit, because it is very difficult to be totally serene and detached when we have first been encouraged to have 'unrealistically' high wishes, to love them passionately and to work very hard for them.

But before you now get discouraged, let me tell you one thing: We are even more at risk of getting frustrated if we are *not* working with manifesting. Our desires are still there and will create a lot of disturbing emotions and, even worse, we might be trying to deaden these feelings with too much alcohol or too much eating. In the worst case scenario we may even get depressed. It is *much* easier to acknowledge our wishes and to learn to let go of our craving. In actual fact:

The process of overcoming our attachment is part of the manifesting process and, as we learn to do that, we will become happier in every aspect of our life.

Only if we feel positive about our wish and we are able to look forward to its fulfilment without any negative feelings have we successfully avoided the pitfall of craving.

When I was younger, it was a complete mystery to me how I could get rid of attachment and craving. I longed for a partner like a shipwrecked person longs for a lifeboat. Many times I got the sympathetic advice from my friends and teachers 'to let go', which drove me totally mad. 'How can I let go of something that I want so badly', I asked and demanded further explanations. But my well-meaning friends couldn't really explain it to me; they just knew that I was blocking the process through my extreme desire. I got this advice from at least ten different people and each time it made me more angry and confused. Eventually, I slowly began to understand.

I knew that one of the most important teachings of

the Buddha says that craving is the root of all suffering and that we have to let it go in order to experience even the most basic happiness. It dawned on me that the Buddha didn't say 'let go of your wishes' - on the contrary, making wishes is an encouraged and valuable practice in Tibetan Buddhism. So, it wasn't the wishes that were the problem; it was only the craving – the negative feelings of greed, impatience and frustration, which often go along with our desires. This insight gave me a lot of relief. At least I didn't have to let go of my wish for a partner - I just had to figure out how to get rid of my negative feelings around my wish.

How can we pursue our wishes passionately while being simultaneously detached? How can we invest our deepest feelings into our desire while completely letting go of control and attachment? The answer to these questions can be found by understanding the yin and yang phases of manifesting.

The yin and yang phases of manifesting

There are two phases in manifesting - the yang or active phase and the yin or receptive phase. The yang phase is the time when we actively work for our wish, whereas in the yin phase we step back and let things happen without interfering anymore. If we look closely we can find many processes that work exactly according to this pattern. The following list shows a few examples of how the yang and yin phases work together and enable us to achieve what we want.

Wish	Yang (active) phase	Yin (receptive) phase	Result
going to sleep	getting ready for bed	stop trying to force sleep and relax	sleep
remember a name	searching our memory	stop trying and relax	remember
growing flowers	sowing the seeds	not digging the seeds up	flowers grow
making friends	showing interest, inviting others	not ringing every day and waiting for return calls	friendship will slowly grow
passing an exam	study hard	getting some sleep, relaxing	retaining our knowledge
attracting customers	doing some advertising	not being too pushy, being patient	customers come
fulfilling our heart-wish	working hard for our wish	letting go of craving, being patient	wish will be fulfilled

We can find the pattern of an active yang and a

receptive yin phase every time we want to make a wish come true. We always have to do something in the beginning to set up the conditions. However, if we do too much it will spoil the process. The more we actively 'try' to fall asleep the less likely we will succeed in doing so. The more often we ring a new friend the more likely it is that we will drive them away. And the more we try to force the process of manifesting the less we will achieve.

But if we don't do anything at all nothing will happen, either. If we want to be successful in making our dreams come true we need to learn the high art of knowing how much to do and when to stop interfering. In other words, skilful manifesting depends on the proper harmony of the yang and the yin phases.

While the yang phase is nothing more than common sense, the yin phase is ultimately a mystery and it would be a mistake to think we are completely in control.

It is exactly this control that we need to surrender in the yin phase and that can be very difficult when we have already worked very hard for our wish.

I once had an interesting conversation with a real estate agent about this very dynamic. The real estate agent had his feet firmly on the ground and I doubt that he had ever heard about something like manifesting. But in his business of selling houses, he deals with making dreams come true all the time. He said to me that nine out of ten sales go through exactly at the moment when people start to give up hope. Over the years, he had noticed that people first put a lot of time and energy into selling and buying a house often with little results. But then they get tired and a bit resigned and they might book a holiday and that is exactly the moment, the real estate agent said, when it all happens. You may have heard similar stories as well, for example about couples who conceived exactly at that moment when they had given up hope.

How to enter the yin phase of manifesting

We don't need to come to the point when we lose hope and start to resign in order to enter the yin phase of manifesting. Instead, we can learn to experience it with joy. How can we do that?

First of all, we need to let go of the idea that the universe owes us something and that we have the perfect right to stamp our foot if it does not deliver our wish quickly. The universe doesn't work like that. It doesn't owe us a nice childhood or a nice partner, nor does it owe us any money or health. Even if we are the only person in the whole world who is poor, ill or unhappy it is us and only us who can sow the seeds of change. But if we keep being sulky about 'the unfairness of it all' we will not be able to manifest our desires and we will invariably end up with a lot of frustration and craving. I know these feelings all too well because I spent years in that kind of misery.

But once we realize that we are in charge of our life, we are on the right track. Then we are ready to let go of the next faulty attitude of trying to control *when* our wish should be fulfilled.

We need to accept that every wish has its own time-scale for coming into existence - just like every seed has its own time-scale for growing into a mature plant. As big plants take longer to grow, big wishes often take longer as well.

When we have accepted that the universe doesn't owe us anything and that we can't control the speed in which our dream will manifest, it will be a whole lot easier to enter the yin phase of manifesting and let go of too much control and craving. In practical terms, this means that we have to let go of our constant obsessing about our wish so that the mysterious process can take place and our wish will manifest 'out of nowhere'.

How do we let go of our impatient thoughts and feelings around our dream without suppressing our dream altogether? How do we let go of our obsessing without forgetting about our wish completely? And how do we manage to finally go to sleep in a sleepless night?

First of all – 'trying to let go' is not the solution. That would be like saying 'try not to think about a pink elephant!' The harder we try *not* to think about the elephant, the more it will appear in our mind.

The same is true if we just *try* not to worry about our wish – we will find that we think about it even more.

What we really need is a change of focus for our mind. We need to find a substitute for our attention that is so interesting that it will successfully distract us while not impeding our wish to come true. What is this substitute focus?

The ultimate way of overcoming our craving is to concentrate on our positive wishes for others.

When we think of our big vision of how others will benefit from our own wish we will be able to let go of our craving much more easily and in that way our wish can manifest. You can try it out – while you focus on the many ways that others will benefit from your wish fulfilment you will rarely get obsessive and impatient. It is in the nature of love to be relaxed and serene. It is exactly for that reason that our loving intention is such a good substitute focus when we have become too impatient.

If we have to do a lot of work to make our wish come true, we face the challenge of bringing the yang and yin phases together into one harmonious movement.

We need to do everything that is necessary to make our wish come true (yang) and be detached and free of craving at the same time (yin). As I have explained, this is most easily achieved through focusing on our contribution to the world. By working in this enjoyable and loving way, we will be able to create enough inner detachment such that the yin phase of manifesting can take place even while we are in the midst of a lot of work.

Attachment and craving are so detrimental to manifesting that we need to do everything we can to let them go. I myself have strong desires and passions and I know how difficult it is, if not impossible, to become totally light-hearted, trusting and wonderfully serene. The good news is that we don't have to overcome our cravings completely. Even if you, like me, maintain a few of your old attachments your wishes can still manifest.

One of my biggest successes with manifesting took place when I managed (unknowingly) to be completely free of craving. It is part of the story that I told you in the introduction. When I visualized my future husband (with quite a bit of craving, I admit) I also visualized that we would live in a beautiful house situated by a lake. The house wasn't really important to me; it just served as a kind of beautiful scenery for my perfect relationship. And through this detached focus I didn't crave for it. As I have already told you, this house manifested in every single detail even though owning such a house was completely impossible where I lived at the time – and obviously I had no idea that it did exist in some foreign country.

Moving into this house that I had visualized for so many years rocked my view of the universe to the core. Never again could I buy into a reality that just consists of what you can see with your ordinary eyes.

Surrender control to your Higher Consciousness

If you have a strong trust in your Higher Consciousness – now is the time for prayer. In the yin phase of manifesting we can hand our wish over to our Higher Consciousness and surrender all control.

But please remember that our Higher Consciousness can't make our wishes come true altogether. If it could, we would all simply pray and receive whatever we want. Unfortunately, we all know that being religious does not guarantee the fulfilment of all our desires. The Higher Power of the universe can only *assist* us in our own efforts.

The more we incorporate genuine love into our personal wishes the closer we come to our Higher Consciousness and the more help we can expect.

The guidance of our Higher Consciousness will come to us through various avenues. Unfortunately, it is unlikely that an angel will knock on our door and hand over the complete instructions for finding our desired aim including a bottle of delicious tasting self-confidence enhancer.

Instead, divine guidance will come to us through ideas, impulses and feelings that feel more or less just like our own. There are moments of sudden clarity, of increased courage and of deep love. Equally, we might be sent a friend or a book that will help us in important ways. If we don't expect to be helped in all these different ways, we can easily dismiss these fleeting moments and wonder why our intuition continues to fail us.

But we can trust that we will be helped. The very fact that we have the ability to love is our connection to our Higher Consciousness.

Seeing life as a school for love and happiness

There is a famous saying that goes something like this: 'Life is hard but once we have accepted that, it isn't hard anymore'. In my opinion, there is a lot of truth in this saying.

A lot of our suffering comes from the unrealistic expectation that everything in our life should go smoothly and pleasantly.

When I was a child I thought that I would always be happy once I was grown up and finally able to escape the hell of my family life. But once I was an adult I had even more problems than I had as a child and I was horrified. Being a grown-up was not at all as nice as I had expected and I felt betrayed, angry and finally depressed. These feelings added an enormous amount of suffering to my already existing problems and made them even more difficult to solve.

Then I encountered Buddhism and learnt that the first noble truth from the Buddha says - freely translated - 'ordinary life is full of suffering.' In the second noble truth the Buddha explains that the human world is full of these frustrations because we always look for happiness in the wrong places.

Learning about these truths relieved me to some extent because I realized that there was nothing wrong with me and my suffering. On the contrary, the Buddha said that suffering was the normal state of the average human. Fortunately, there was light at the end of the tunnel because the third and the fourth noble truths explain that there is a way to end our suffering through the awakening of our loving heart.

When these teachings slowly trickled into my mind, a shift in my attitude towards the world took place. Instead of being angry and full of self-pity, I saw my life with all its problems as a big classroom in a school for love and happiness. Problems were no longer only a nuisance but started to be the daily bread of my schoolwork, which I could accept more willingly. And the way to pass my exams was to develop more equanimity, love and happiness. For me, it is definitely true that life isn't so hard since I accepted that it is hard.

If we see the time of our unfulfilled wish as nothing other than a nuisance, we block the process of making our wishes come true and we also miss out on the great opportunity to learn about the way the universe works.

The times in our lives when we *don't* have what we want are actually the most precious times because we are forced to find in our own hearts the fulfilment and the happiness that we normally expect from outside sources. When we are lonely, poor, ill and unfulfilled, we can learn to find in the depth of our heart a source of happiness that is totally independent of our outer conditions. And it is this unconditional happiness that will ultimately liberate us from all our suffering.

The most important thing to learn in times of deprivation is to love ourselves like a caring parent would love their only child.

Even if our child is not the brightest and most beautiful we still love her or him intensely. We will give them the best food, a good education and lots of affection. In the same way, we need to love ourselves: We must not criticize ourselves in a demeaning way, we must not say horrible things to ourselves and we must not give up on ourselves – ever. Instead, we envelop ourselves in a bubble of loving light, no matter how hard our life is, no matter how many setbacks we experience and no matter how many people reject us. The Buddha said, 'We, ourselves, as much as anybody in the entire universe, deserve our love and affection.'

I give the following exercise routinely to all my clients and it has never failed to bring positive results. Even the most self-loathing person softened when trying it and felt much better very quickly. But the exercise will only work if you do it on a regular basis.

Exercise: Developing more love for yourself
(to be done as often as you need)

Remember a moment in your life when you deeply loved someone. You might have felt this love for your

> baby, your partner or even a pet.
>
> **When** you feel this love, just turn it towards yourself without thinking about it a lot and without changing it. Feel love for yourself just as much as you loved the other person.
>
> **Start** to talk to yourself in the same loving way that you would talk to someone you love deeply. Speak about your problems and wishes in a compassionate, soothing way like you would talk to a small, unhappy child.
>
> **Do** this exercise frequently and in many situations until it becomes second nature.

If we can love ourselves we will find it much easier to develop the same kind of feelings towards others because we realize that everybody wants to be treated in that way. And that is exactly the moment when the positive circle of karma is set into motion because the love and appreciation we give to others will invariably come back to us at some point.

Focus on having fun

In order to prise our mind successfully away from our constant craving and worrying around our wish, we need a strong and attractive replacement focus. In my experience, simply having fun is another good way to give us this distraction. Seriousness is the precursor of rigidity and then nothing can move. Instead, we should pursue the process of manifesting like a great game that is really fun to play. The frame of mind that we had as children when we were happily playing pretend-games is the best frame of mind for making our dreams come true, as well.

Unfortunately, not everybody is able to play as happily as an unconcerned child. But what we *can* do is to focus on the bits of our manifesting process that are fun. For instance, even if we don't like doing presentations at work, we might enjoy wearing smart clothes. So we could concentrate on the pleasure of that. And even if we do not like going on blind-dates, we can focus on the fun of having a drink in a nice bar. We should also try to develop as much humour as possible.

Manifesting can grind to a complete halt if we allow our negative outlook to take over and cracking a few jokes about it all can shatter these walls of rigidity.

This is something I learnt that from my first Buddhist teacher who never allowed his students to talk about their problems in a serious way. When we wanted to tell him about our problems and unfulfilled dreams we had to take a guitar and sing to him. Imagine that! At that point in my life I frequently felt quite desperate. I was so lonely, I was so afraid and I had very little hope that things could get better. And I had to sing about it all and make a tragic-comedy out of it! To be honest, for me that worked like a miracle drug. Once I overcame my initial resistance to ridicule my suffering, I started to take it less and less seriously. More and more often, in the middle of the tears I burst out laughing. I just couldn't buy into this tragic show anymore. Not long afterwards my attacks of desperation stopped altogether.

Being grateful

In order to enter the yin-phase of manifesting we can focus on our altruistic offer, on having fun, on handing over our wish to our Higher Power, on loving ourselves and on developing self-deprecating humour. If any of that works for you – great.

But if you still struggle with negative feelings around your unfulfilled wish you could also try the gratefulness exercise. In neuro-linguistic programming (NLP), there is a technique called 'reframing' and it means putting a positive frame around something that we usually consider as negative. In the good old days, this was called 'every cloud has a silver lining'. No matter how we call this technique, the gratefulness exercise is another excellent way to help us stop obsessing about our wish.

The gratefulness exercise was the turning point in my life. It helped me more than anything else to take my mind off my inner and outer negativity and redirect it on to something I felt genuinely positive about. And it is such a simple practice that it hardly deserves the title 'exercise'. But for the sake of clarity, I present it here as an exercise.

The gratefulness exercise (to be done daily if we experience a lot of craving)

Firstly, think about all the positive things in your life including those you normally take for granted, for example, the fact that you live in a free country or that your legs are working. Say out loud, 'I am grateful…' and add one of these positive things. Then focus on your gratefulness until you can feel a lovely feeling in your heart.

Once you feel some real gratefulness say to yourself, 'I am grateful for…' and then add the first thing that comes to your mind. This doesn't need to be something positive; you can equally add something you feel bad about. ('I am grateful that my partner was so awful to me yesterday…')

Then finish your sentence with '…because…' and add a genuine reason why you are grateful. ('I am grateful that my partner was so awful to me yesterday because it forces me to make a decision about whether we should stay together.')

Go on in this fashion for five to ten minutes. Repeat over and over 'I am grateful for…' add the first thought that comes to your mind, no matter whether it is positive or negative and find a genuine reason for your gratefulness.

Do this exercise frequently until it becomes second nature.

I used to do this exercise for several years as part of my bathroom routine first thing in the morning. As a result I usually turned up at work in a pretty good mood. After all, there was nothing left in my life that I could grumble about. I was grateful for *everything!* This exercise only feels contrived when we start doing it. Once we are in the swing of it, we will quickly realize that there is indeed something to be genuinely grateful for in everything.

As you read in the introduction, I did not have the proverbial happy childhood but more or less the opposite. However, I am grateful for this experience because it led me to develop in the way I did. Not having the parental love that so many people take for granted, I was forced to rely on my inner resources. The suffering of my childhood and young adulthood was certainly not nice and I do not wish it on anybody. But for me it was the gateway into a more empowered life and for that I am deeply grateful.

Give yourself a break

The last piece of advice about letting go of craving is to take regular breaks from the manifesting process. Making our wishes come true doesn't depend solely on ourselves and we don't need to be totally in control of the whole process. On the contrary, if we have done our bit we need to get out of the way! So we need to step back and allow the mystery of things 'popping' into existence to take place.

Even if you are not sure whether you have done enough to make your wish come true, take regular 'manifesting holidays'. Meet friends, pursue a hobby or – if possible - take a real vacation.

Action plan for step five

The most important action that you need to take now is:

If you feel craving for your wish let it go in the way that works best for you.

Step six
Dealing with the waiting time

If you ask me how long it will take to make your dream come true I can tell you that manifesting works instantly – in a way. As soon as we utter our wish the whole universe conspires and works on its fulfillment. Unfortunately, this 'preparation' can take some time. How long this time will be, nobody knows for sure - it might go very quickly or it might take a little longer.

In my experience, it is those wishes which are a challenge to our deep-seated beliefs that take the longest.

One of our deepest beliefs is how much love and happiness is possible for us and it is not easy to increase our trust that we could have *much* more happiness and *much* more love in our life. Can you believe that you could make *much* more money in a job in which you are *much* happier and in which you can bring *much* more happiness to other people? It's a challenging thought for most of us.

In my own life the time from making a wish until it came true varied from a few weeks to several years. I see the same pattern in my clients. I've had several clients who were unhappy singles for decades – but within weeks of clearing out their unconscious mind, as described in step two, they fell in love with a very suitable and loving person. In other cases, it has taken a few months and in yet others cases even longer.

The fulfilment of our wishes depends on so many factors that it is impossible to foretell when they will finally manifest. First of all, there are always other people involved in our dreams - and they can't be controlled. If we want to buy a farm in the countryside, for instance, the people who live there at the moment need to be ready to move out. This again will depend on a lot of factors in their own lives. The strings of involvements to make our own personal wish come true are actually endless and it is really a miracle when finally everything falls into place. How long that will take nobody can tell and many wishes involve a shorter or a longer period of waiting.

If we want to get a book published, for example, we can write it rather quickly and send it off to some publishers. However, after that we have to *wait*. Then we might get a lot of rejections and send our manuscript to even more publishers. Then we have to *wait* again. Annoying, isn't it?

The waiting time can be a big challenge and we can perceive it as a test that shows us whether or not we have learnt our previous lessons of manifesting.

If we start to complain about the unfairness that 'every idiot' can get what they want whereas we are completely ignored, we need to repeat step five: letting go of our craving.

If we get discouraged and we want to give up on our

wish, we need to repeat step one: finding our heart-wish.

If we interpret rejections as a sign from the universe that our dream is 'not meant to be', we need to remind ourselves that we are not trying to get the best from an already existing reality but that we can actually *create our own reality*.

The truth is that the universe is not in charge of our life – nobody is, unless we put someone else in charge. *We ourselves* are the one and only guiding force in our life. No matter how many bad omens we seem to perceive, no matter how many unfortunate coincidences seem to block our way, *we* can make our wishes come true by painstakingly working with all eight steps of manifesting. Quite often this will involve a period of waiting, which we have to accept patiently and we need to resist the impulse to plunge into hopelessness or frustration. This waiting time is not just an empty stretch which is nothing but a nuisance. The contrary is true.

The time that we are waiting for the fulfillment of our wish can be a time of enormous inner growth.

We are opening up to a much bigger vision than we ever thought possible. We are developing the muscles of our wish-power and we are becoming much more loving and giving through focusing on the altruistic side of our wish. In other words, while working with manifesting we are growing personally and spiritually more than ever.

All we need to do while we are waiting is to go patiently through all the previous steps of manifesting and make sure that we are applying them in the right way. Here is a short check-list of the previous steps of manifesting:

Step one:
Is our heart-wish bold and exciting and do we focus on how we want to contribute to the world with our wish?

Step two:
Do we clear out our unconscious mind of any resistance by regularly practicing the appropriate exercises?

Step three:
Do we work in an organized and intuitive way for our wish and do we accept any kind of help that is available to us?

Step four:
Do we regularly practice the chakra meditation and maintain our 'emotional goal-vibration' as much as possible.

Step five:
Do we patiently let go of our craving and frustration each time they arise?

If all these things are in place it is only a matter of time until our wish will come true. But please don't think that you have to be perfect to make your wishes come true. Even if you are experiencing cravings, even if you feel hopeless and despairing at times and even if you don't always do enough to make your wish come true, it won't matter so much as long as you can return again and again to a more appropriate attitude.

We are all on our way and nobody is a finished product. It is important that we allow ourselves to make mistakes and see ourselves as a learner in our field rather than expecting to be perfect and then not trying at all. I have made plenty of these mistakes myself and I often still do. It does not seem to matter too much and only if my mistakes become too obvious do I tell myself, 'Tara, if you want to write clever books about manifesting, you should at least *try* to adhere to your own rules yourself!'

It is helpful to think of a wish as a seed that has its own predetermined time to germinate, grow and finally flower. We need to nurture and care for our seedling but there is nothing we can do to make our plant flower much earlier than it is meant to do.

Some wishes come true within days and others take a nerve-wrecking amount of time even though we obey all the instructions of manifesting to the letter.

I know from my own experience that we often can't appreciate that there is a perfect timing for each wish when we are in the middle of our manifesting process. 'Why did I not get this great job?' we moan and we feel tempted to throw our wish-fulfilling gem against the wall to make it more obedient. However, our jewel will not be impressed by our tyrannical behavior, so it is best to control our temper.

In many cases, only after we have received our wish can we understand why everything took so long and why we had to endure all the puzzling twists and turns.

Many years ago, I was working in a job that was limited to twelve months and so I had to look for another one during that year. My chances were good because there were quite a few jobs available in my field. So I applied – and was rejected. I applied again, was accepted – and lost the job at the last minute because there was an internal application that had priority. In that manner, it went on for several months and I got more rejections than I had ever received before. I was confused and frustrated.

Then a good friend of mine told me about a job vacancy in her office and I was thrilled. 'This is my dream job' I rejoiced. 'Now I know why I got all these other rejections – I was meant to work with my dear friend!' I applied and the boss of her company was really enthusiastic about me – bit I was rejected shortly afterwards because of internal politics that were beyond the influence of everybody involved. I tell you, now I was really frustrated because I couldn't understand why the world had conspired against me. In the end, I became unemployed despite a whole year of searching for a job in a pretty good work market. But strangely, despite my job-plight, my mood was better than ever.

Then came the moment when I finally started to

understand the 'reason' behind my mishap. Only two weeks after my job had finished I met my future husband and within days we both knew that I would move to England to be with him. As you can see, everything was perfect timing although I hadn't been able to understand it while I was in the middle of this process.

How to deal with setbacks

Freely estimated, from a thousand people only one hundred embark on the journey to make bold wishes come true. From those hundred 99 experience setbacks and 90 people give up after the first or second problem because they just can't take the frustration anymore. So, in the end, only ten out of a thousand people will successfully achieve major changes in their lives.

I find these numbers quite sad. Our wishes are bound to be fulfilled because this is the way the universe works and still so many people give up and continue to live mediocre or even miserable existences because they do not trust the manifesting process deeply enough.

In my personal research about who is most successful in making their wishes come true, I have come to the conclusion that there are two sorts of people who have a distinct advantage. The first group comprises those rare individuals who have an unshakeable sunny and optimistic attitude, which they apply to all of their endeavors. And through their positive mood they are very capable of dealing with frustrations and setbacks elegantly. Unfortunately, there are not many of these indestructible optimists around.

The other group with an advantage is very different. These are people who experienced a lot of suffering and hardship early on in their lives and I have found that many of them have a great amount of resilience and are well equipped to deal with setbacks and frustrations later on in life. Therefore, they usually make up a significant proportion of the ten people who succeed with manifesting.

When I started to work as a drugs counselor, I expected that most of my clients had childhoods full of abuse and neglect that had driven them into their self-destructive drug habit. How surprised I was to find that in many cases this was not true! I worked for years with addicts and their parents and found that in many cases it wasn't abuse and neglect that drove people into addiction - it was more or less the opposite: over-protection and over-caring. More than once I visited a thirty-something addict in their home where they lived with their parents who cooked for them, cleaned up after them and regularly provided them with money for their drug-habit.

If we were very spoilt as children we need to understand that the ease and comfort of our childhood is not likely to continue into our adult life unless we learn to persevere despite setbacks and frustrations.

We are always better off accepting that life is hard and putting on our sturdy walking-boots to scramble over all of life's obstacles. Then, and only then, will we be able to deal with the possible setbacks in manifesting and make our biggest wishes come true.

Some people who start working with the manifesting process feel puzzled about the fact that they experience rejections and setbacks at all. 'Shouldn't this method lead me straight to my desired aim?' they wonder. Well, manifesting *would* lead us to our wish straightaway if we would only allow it. But because we get so attached to all the possibilities which are *not* the fulfillment of our dream these possibilities will reject *us*. Manifesting is a wonderful double-sided sword because it works in two ways:

Manifesting attracts what we want and *repulses* whatever is not in alignment with our wish. What seems to be a rejection might actually serve the perfect fulfillment of our dream.

Do you remember all the rejections I got when I looked for a job? They were actually serving me well because just around the next corner was waiting my husband-to-be and with him the possibility to work self-employed. As I have already told you, I visualized being self-employed for many years – without ever seeing any possibility of achieving this dream. Therefore, my own visualization had taken away from me all the possibilities of getting yet another employed job. Instead, it had manifested what I really wanted – the possibility of being self-employed.

If you look for your soulmate and you wonder why you get more rejections than ever – now you know the reason. You will reject or *be rejected* by any potential partner who doesn't completely fit your wish-list. This happens whether you are aware of the disadvantages of someone or not. Like myself, you might think you have found the dream person or the dream job only to find that some hidden disadvantage destroys this possibility. This is not the universe trying to punish you – it is your own deep wish that has deterred what is not totally in alignment with your wish-list. Here is a list of helpful do's and don'ts in case you experience setbacks in your manifesting process:

Setbacks and rejections - Do's

Tell yourself: *'I am only experiencing this setback because there is something better for me.'* This is not just a cheap consolation but the truth. Manifesting *does* work and the reason that we didn't get what we thought was a good opportunity is that it wasn't in total alignment with our wish-list. A client of mine was distraught that he couldn't buy a certain apartment only to find three months later that there was a major noise problem in that house and that he would have been very unhappy there.

View your setbacks as lessons and try to learn from them. Did you try to force something? Were you about to make a bad compromise? Could you have avoided this disappointment if you had been more scrutinizing?

When you experience setbacks and disappointments repeat like a mantra: 'Whatever is for the highest good of all beings, may it happen.'

If you feel very hurt and disappointed by your setback, focus on the exercises outlined in step four - raising your vibration.

Carry on with visualizing and working for your dream as usual.

Setbacks and rejections - Don'ts

Don't try to manipulate people you know by visualizing that they make decisions in your favor. I know it is tempting but it would be trying to force your will on to others, which will be detrimental in the long term. We should never try to manipulate a specific person with our psychic powers into calling us, feeling sexually attracted to us or buying our products. Instead, we should focus on our wish in an unspecific way and visualize finding *a* partner or *lots* of customers without specifying who exactly these people are.

Don't give up. Setbacks are not a sign from the universe to tell you that your wish is doomed or that it is 'not meant to be'. On the contrary, setbacks are a sign that there is something better for you in store. As you continue using the exercises in this book, your intuition will become clearer and you will become more able to find your aim in a more direct way with fewer setbacks. When I first tried to get published, I received seventy rejections and it would have been very sad if I had given up by thinking 'it is not meant to be' because, nearly a year later, I suddenly received six letters from interested publishers within one week.

Don't change and limit your wish out of frustration. If you always wanted to be an artist don't try to tell yourself that it is much more desirable to become an accountant, instead. You will gain nothing if you try to talk yourself into wanting something that your parents or your church might think is a good idea but what is *not* what you want in your heart of hearts. Instead, stick with your heart-wish, even if you have no idea how you could ever realize it. If you regularly visualize your aim and accept every help that is available then you will be surprised how much support you can get.

One of my more recent wishes was to buy a new house with my husband and I was very confident when we started our search because I considered myself a 'manifesting expert'. However, I have been taught a big lesson about getting overconfident because I have never encountered more setbacks than during our trials to buy this house. After nearly one and half years of intense searching, I finally started to lose my confidence. 'How can I write a book about manifesting' I thought miserably, 'if I can't even find a house?' Not only was my move at stake but also my reputation as the 'manifesting expert'!

Then a beautiful house appeared in the newspaper and some light of hope appeared at the end of the tunnel. We viewed it and instantly we 'knew' that this was it – our dream house. We made an offer and we were very happy. However, after three days our deal fell through because the vendor wanted to sell the house to someone else. My mood hit rock-bottom. (So much for being a manifesting expert!)

After a while, I made some half-hearted attempts to put my own lessons into practice and I tried to tell myself that this was only happening because there was a better house for us and that our 'dream house' might have some hidden disadvantages that I wasn't aware of. But despite my trying, I just couldn't believe this. This house had the perfect size, garden and location and there were definitely no similar houses nearby. I even toyed with the idea of visualizing that the deal of those other buyers would fall through, as well. (But I didn't do it, honestly!)

When I analyzed my situation further I came to the conclusion that all this was teaching me another lesson in humility. Considering myself an expert didn't mean that I was completely in control and I had to learn to acknowledge the fact that the actual 'magic' of manifesting is beyond anybody's control. So I calmed down, regained my good mood and kept trying to find a new house by focusing on how I could enjoy the house search and on how I could contribute to all beings through our purchase.

Believe it or not, after only two weeks there was a most wonderful house for sale, not even two hundred yards away from the previous one, which was a lot cheaper and which had a much more beautiful garden. We viewed it, we made an offer – and we were told that there was so much interest in this house that the real estate agent would auction it off! But by now I had learnt my lesson and so I just repeated the mantra, 'whatever is in the best interest of all beings, may it happen…whatever is in the best interest of all beings, may it happen.'

When I called the estate agent again a few days later, he told me that the auction was cancelled and that we could probably have the house if we raised our offer to a certain price. This price was still well within our limits and this is how we got our dream house number two.

The moral: even 'manifesting experts' are only human beings with lots of flaws.

Developing serenity and peace of mind

In many respects manifesting can be compared with drilling a tunnel through a mountain. In the beginning, when our wish is new and exciting, we just have soft soil and we will make good progress. But, when we have tried for a long time with only small results, we have arrived in the middle of the mountain where we often find nothing but granite. Many people now make the mistake of turning around and starting a new hole (a new wish) only to find themselves confronted with the same granite a little later.

This image of the tunnel tells us that we should not waste our time scraping shallow dents into the mountainside by constantly changing our wishes but keep with the same wish no matter how hard it is. I know how difficult this can be because I myself have been there many times.

Unfortunately, even though we have instant coffee, instant Internet banking and all the other devices which help us to get what we want faster and faster, we can't reduce the time of manifesting any more than we can reduce the time that it takes to be pregnant and deliver a baby.

With pregnancy there is no option of giving up. We have to see it through, no matter how tired we are and no matter how scared we are. In the same way, we have to stick with our wish and, as surely as we will deliver a baby when we are pregnant, we can look forward to the fulfillment of our wish when we work with manifesting. It just might take some time.

Patience is a virtue that isn't very popular these days and I am not a friend of it either. I really wish I knew a way to make wishes come true more instantaneously as I am very impatient myself. However, I do understand that patience is a virtue because it protects us from a host of negative feelings created by greed and the inability to wait. So, no matter whether we like or dislike the idea of patience, we are all better off developing some of it.

A good friend of mine also reminded me that if all

our wishes came true instantaneously we might be in a lot of trouble. All the negative thoughts we might be thinking involuntarily would immediately manifest, which would not be a good scenario! He is of course right.

Unfortunately, it is impossible to know the 'due-date' of when our wish should manifest. But our success with manifesting depends a great deal on how much we are able *not* to become impatient and frustrated. Our attitude must be like this: 'If my wish doesn't come true this year then it is fine that it will arrive next year. And if it is not next year, I am happy to get what I want the year after. And if it is not, then I am happy to wait even longer.'

If we can look at our desires in this way there will be no unfulfilled wishes anymore. There will be no more 'I tried but it didn't work', because there will only be wishes that aren't fulfilled *yet.* But if we are like most people, we might find it difficult to develop this amount of serenity and, in that case, it might be helpful to review step five 'Overcoming craving'.

We can only be successful in manifesting when we master living with our unfulfilled wish without becoming so frustrated that we want to change it or to give it up.

Sometimes people mistake patience and serenity for not really engaging with their wish or for not really wanting it. This is a faulty attitude, as well. We need to wish for our desired aim as passionately as described in steps one and two *and* we need to be serene at the same time. Imagine holding a string in your hand which leads you to your wish. You have to maintain a certain tension. If you pull too hard on your string you have fallen into the pitfall of craving and if you let the string slacken you are too disengaged.

The perfect way of working with manifesting is to fix our string in our heart and maintain a gentle tension that gives us a pleasurable tug in our heart that pulls us in the right direction.

Action plan for step six

The most important action that you need to take now is:

Know how to deal with setbacks and rejections in case you experience these problems.

Resist the temptation to give up on your wish once the going gets tough.

Step seven
Removing any remaining obstacles

In the previous steps we have explored the six main elements of manifesting our desires. In step seven we will be dealing with any obstacles that may still be in the way of manifesting our wish. Unfortunately, if we are imprisoned in addictions or in destructive relationships, if our mind is poisoned with guilt, resentment and self-pity, we will find it hard to accomplish the previous six steps of manifesting.

The following sections will offer help to eliminate these problems. But if these issues are very persistent it may also be useful to see a therapist or join a self-help group. Another possibility is to practice Higher-Consciousness healing that is explained in my book *The Five-Minute Miracle*. Higher-Consciousness healing is an extremely simple and effective self-help method to overcome deep-seated psychological problems.

Passively putting up with negativity

From all the possible obstacles in manifesting, the obstacle of 'not wishing' is by far the most detrimental. As we have already discussed, we can't be without wishes. So, if people are in a terrible job or in a soul-destroying marriage and yet they don't actively work for change, they are wishing on a deeper and unconscious level that things should stay as they are.

The worst obstacle in manifesting is not wishing at all.

One of the most common reasons that keeps people from wishing for a better life is the fear of being disappointed if they fail. 'If I wish for better health or a better career and I don't get it', they might say, 'I will feel even worse than if I hadn't wished for it at all. Once my desire is awakened it will bother me much more if I don't get what I want.'

There is some truth in this argument. Once we set our heart on something it will be much harder to stay serene and detached compared with never wanting something in the first place. But the solution is not putting up with a mediocre or even bad life. The solution is to wish only for those things that are really worthwhile and will definitely bring us happiness. And once we have chosen our heart-wish, we can relax because we can rely on the second truth of manifesting: 'we *will* get what we want'. If we stay with our dream in a committed way without getting angry and frustrated it *will* manifest at some point because this is the way the universe works.

Unsupportive relationships

One of my own biggest obstacles for making my wishes come true was relating and even clinging to people who weren't really supportive of me and who certainly didn't wish that I achieve the happiness that I have now. Weird, isn't it? Why should anybody maintain relationships with people who are not really loving and supportive? Good question. Now that I have all that behind me, I wonder about it myself.

The answer is as simple as it is sad. Most people who are stuck in unsupportive relationships are very afraid of being alone. Just like myself, they do not realize that being alone is much more strengthening than being with an unsupportive partner. They may even find it hard to imagine being treated with ongoing love and respect. 'You can't expect never having conflicts!' they may say. No, I don't expect never having conflicts but I do expect to argue with my partner without hostile feelings and while continuing to love each other.

The quality of our most important relationships is the direct outcome of our most dearly held (and possibly unconscious) beliefs. And our relationships are the fertile field, so to speak, on which all our other wishes can grow.

The emotional atmosphere of our primary relationships will dictate how we feel in all other areas of our life, no matter how successful we are and no matter how much we meditate.

Unfortunately, we cannot just blame our partner if we are not successful with manifesting because our relationship with this person *is still* our own wish. If we want to change a negative relationship there is only one way: we need to wish for a more loving relationship. We need to stick to our wish and we need to do all we can to make it happen while keeping in mind that we can't change our partner against their will. In other words, we need to take the risk that our unsupportive relationship will break up and that we will have to go a part of our journey alone until we find someone who is more loving. This is exactly what I did and I can reassure you that it was absolutely worth it.

If we do have to break up with someone, it is paramount that we always maintain a loving and forgiving attitude and send the other person away with our blessing. If we maintain grudges and resentments, we will not be able to leave the other person entirely behind. They will still be tied to us in an invisible way and will keep holding us back. Only love will set us free.

The exercise described in the next section about moving out of family traps can be used to let go of all negative feelings with former partners, as well.

Moving out of family traps

It is possible to break up with a partner who is unsupportive of our aims but we can never break up with our original family. Even if we move to another continent and never communicate with them again, we are still bound to our family by invisible ties that may hold us back. For example, certain family values may be lodged deep within our unconscious mind and dictate much of our beliefs even if we consciously rebel against them. This is the reason why so many people end up with a partner who is so similar to one of their parents - even if they have negative feelings towards this parent.

The following exercise is designed to explore unconscious family barriers and then to let them go.

Exercise: Receive the blessing of your entire family

Imagine your two parents and two sets of grandparents are in front of you. Even if you have never met some of these relatives, imagine that they are there. Also, add anybody who was an important parent figure for you in your childhood.

One by one, tell each of your relatives about your wish and ask them for their blessing.

Sense whether your relative is happy to give you their blessing or if they have any objections.

If they support your dream, imagine them standing behind you and strengthening your back.

If you sense that your relative has any objections send loving light to them and wish them to be happy from the bottom of your heart. Imagine that if they were happy they would want you to be happy as well and support you in making your dreams come true.

Imagine your unsupportive relative enveloped in a bubble of loving light and floating away in the distance with your blessing.

Continue sending love to your unsupportive relative for at least two weeks twice daily.

Repeat this exercise with each relative who is unsupportive several times.

Letting go of jealously and envy

In Buddhism, feelings like jealously and envy are called poisons of the mind and even the most perfect life can be poisoned through these negative emotions because there is always someone who has something better. Unfortunately, envy and jealousy are also major obstacles for our manifesting practice because they cloud the space into which our dream could manifest.

If we suffer from jealously, first of all we need to admit these feelings to ourselves and not pretend that we are above them. Then we need to forgive ourselves and envelop ourselves with a bubble of loving light, just like a mother would envelop her child with love and comfort.

In the next step we imagine that the person who we envy may be just as envious themselves because there is no perfect situation for any human being. Even if someone is beautiful, their body could always be improved in many ways. Even if someone is rich, they may still have many unfulfilled desires. And even if someone has a wonderful career, there are always others who are doing far better. So, if the person we envy doesn't feel jealous of others themselves, it isn't for the reason that they just 'have everything'. Freedom from envy and jealousy is a state of mind that can be achieved by everybody independently of how much they have.

One of the best ways to overcome jealousy is to see the person who has so much more than we have as

a model or a teacher.

If we can appreciate and even admire the qualities of this person we can open ourselves to their energy field and in that way we will be able to participate in their good qualities. We can then develop these qualities in ourselves much more easily and achieve for ourselves what they have. For instance, if we envy someone who is very attractive, this negative feeling will work like poison in our mind and will make us even less attractive ourselves. But if we can genuinely admire this person, some of their positive qualities will mysteriously pass into us – and we will become more attractive ourselves in the process.

This is not just esoteric hocus-pocus – try it out – it works! Whenever you envy someone – if you can genuinely admire their qualities, you are then developing them in yourself at that very moment! The more you can do that, the more positive qualities you will receive from this person. In this way, jealously will be transformed from a poison of your mind into a genuine friend.

Overcoming resentment

Resentment and smoldering grudges represent some of the biggest obstacles for our wishes to come true. Why is that? Why can't we be angry with some people without losing our ability to make our own wishes come true?

The answer is that our personal universe arises out of the space of our mind. If this space is filled, even partially, with anger and resentment (no matter how much these feelings seem to be justified) our universe will be poisoned by this emotion and we will not be able to manifest something that will make us deeply happy.

I have many clients who wish for a soulmate. Virtually all of them have lingering resentments towards an ex-partner or a parent. Once we remove these grudges many of my clients move on to find a partner within a few months.

Unfortunately, many people do not realize how much they hinder themselves by their lingering resentments.

Grudges towards parents have the most detrimental effect. Our bonds with our parents are so deep and complex that we will never be able to escape them. Therefore, if we continue to be angry with one of our parents we subtly hate ourselves and in that way we will never be able to achieve real happiness.

It is a real shame that some therapies encourage people to forcefully express their anger towards their (imaginary) parents because this actually increases the anger instead of dissolving it. The real solution is learning to forgive and let go of our old grudges.

Forgiveness does *not* mean condoning the behavior of the person who has hurt us. And it does *not* mean taking away their guilt. Forgiveness simply means that we stop harboring grudges and resentment.

Instead, we simply wish our parents to be happy and

imagine that if they had been happy they would have been more loving and caring - they would not have done anything neglectful or hurtful to us. By making these good wishes, a deep healing process is set into motion that frees us entirely from the problems caused by any form of past trauma. I have worked in this way with myself and with numerous clients and I can promise you that it brings complete and lasting healing from the most terrible traumas from our past.

Wishing someone who has hurt us to be happy does not necessarily mean being close to them. Only after we have received a sincere apology can we be close again. In all other cases, we need to let this person go with our blessing. The following exercise shows how we can rid ourselves of any resentment that is still poisoning our life and hampering our manifesting process.

Exercise: Letting go of old grudges (to be done as often as we need it)

Start by wishing yourself to be happy and enveloping yourself with love like a loving parent would comfort a child. Once you can feel a loving feeling for yourself, go to the next step.

See in your mind the person who has hurt or neglected you.

Say to this person, *'(Name), although I still don't condone what you did, I stop resenting you and wish you to be happy.'* See in your mind how the other

> person becomes soft and remorseful when enveloped in your loving wishes. Then send this person away with your blessing.
>
> **If possible**, write or speak to this person and let them know that you do not harbor any bad feelings towards them anymore and that you wish them all the best.

I believe that our potential for compassion and forgiveness is much bigger than we usually experience. I have heard several reports of Tibetans who had endured torture from their Chinese occupiers while continuously maintaining a compassionate attitude towards them. These Tibetans believed deeply in the law of karma, which dictates that everybody will get back what they give out, and they even felt sorry for their torturers because they knew that they were creating the most terrible future for themselves.

Overcoming Self-pity

Most feelings of resentment are accompanied by feelings of self-pity because we feel so victimized and unfairly treated. Self-pity feels like a natural response to such treatment. But if we want to be successful we need to stop believing that we can't manifest our dreams because something awful has happened to us in the past. No matter how justified this attitude appears – it is *not* true! I can attest for this with my own experiences and all the experiences of my clients. Even people who have experienced the most terrible traumas in the past were able to leave them entirely behind with the forgiveness exercise of the previous section.

Also, if we read the biographies of very successful people, it is amazing how many of them came from very hard or disadvantaged backgrounds and how many of them suffered great losses in their lives. But, instead of drowning in self-pity, these people manifested great successes, instead.

The best way to emulate these inspiring people is to transform our self-pity into self-love. This requires only a little twist in our attitude because self-pity is really a distorted form of self-love. Once we can love ourselves we will feel more energy and optimism and then we can start creating the conditions for our success.

In order to turn self-pity into self-love, imagine how we would comfort an unhappy child. Surely we wouldn't *just* pity her. We would comfort her lovingly but then we would get up and do something to help her. In the same way, we need to love and comfort ourselves but then we have to get up in order to change our detrimental circumstances. All change starts within – so the best place to start is practicing the exercises outlined in this book.

Overcoming Guilt

If there is something in your past that produces guilt - like hurting, betraying or harming others - it is an obstacle that stands in the way of making your wishes come true.

This is not because God wants to punish you but because your own bad conscience (even if this is completely unconscious) will not allow you to achieve greater happiness in life.

As a therapist, I have observed this dynamic numerous times and I have also experienced this in my own life. It is our own guilt-feelings that block our success.

When I worked as a drugs counselor, I worked both with battered wives and with their violent counterparts. I quickly realized that the aggressive, violent men were in a far worse position. It is a myth to believe that we can do awful things to others and then live a happy life. If this seems to be the case, one can only see a very superficial layer of the truth. As a counselor, I had the opportunity to talk to people who had done really bad things to others and I always found these people to be extremely unhappy.

One example was a university professor who had killed somebody in a car accident but had been bailed out by an expensive solicitor. Even though the professor knew that he had caused the accident out of carelessness, he did not receive any punishment at all. Shortly after this happened, the professor started drinking excessively to the extent that it destroyed his career and his marriage. This is an extreme example of someone punishing themselves but I have seen similar dynamics with everyone who has hurt others in the past.

In order to get rid of our unconscious intention to punish ourselves for our own wrong-doing, we need to sift through our past actions and examine whether anybody got hurt – or would have been hurt if they had known what we did.

If possible, we should apologize and repair things as much as possible. But if contacting the people who we have harmed would cause even more hurt, we need to find a way to make things good in a more hidden way. We can pray for people, we can send them love or we can give money to charity on their behalf. When all this is done, we need to forgive ourselves and then we will be free to manifest the happy life our dreams.

Overcoming Regret

The little brother of guilt is regret which means, for instance, ongoing grief for a breakdown of a relationship or a bankruptcy of a business. These feelings of regret are a mixture of grief, guilt and melancholic longing that things should have been otherwise. Such feelings can be a big hindrance for making a new beginning and fulfilling our wishes.

If you suffer from regret, you need to practice loving and forgiving yourself on a regular basis, as explained in the previous exercise.

Try to realize that you do not benefit anybody if you keep yourself from becoming happy again, least of all your children if you have any.

Children always learn best from models. If we can show them how to get through a major trauma in life and get out the other side with our spirit intact, we will help them tremendously to cope with the traumas that they might have to face one day.

Don't punish yourself if you had a major break-up by henceforth living a minimal life. Remember the words of the Buddha 'We, ourselves, as much as anybody in the entire universe, deserve our love and affection'.

Too much chaos, clutter and distraction

If someone is up to their neck in chaos, clutter and distraction it will be hard to find the focus of mind that is necessary to be successful with manifestation techniques. Here are a few suggestions that may be helpful to overcome this problem.

Generally speaking, people only do things if they assume (consciously or unconsciously) that at the bottom line they are getting something out of it. So, if we find ourselves surrounded by so much chaos, clutter and distraction that we can't find any space to work for our wish, we need to ask ourselves what we are getting out of this situation. For example, having lots of chaos around us might protect us from being bored, from feeling useless and from the 'big black hole' in which we could suddenly disappear if we don't keep ourselves constantly occupied.

Having lots of dependent people around us who eat up the last of our energy reserves may protect us from looking in the mirror and answering the difficult question, 'who am I and what do I want in this world?' Spending too much time in front of the television may help us to take our mind off the fear that arises when we think of the next step to make our wish come true.

Once we understand how all the chaos and stress of our life serves us on a deeper level, we can let it go bit by bit.

A good place to start is tidying up our home. We could then try to tidy up our daily to-do list and do only those things for others that they really can't do for themselves. In the last step, we need to tidy up our relationships and only relate closely to those people who are totally supportive of our aims.

It is probably not easy to do all this tidying up and a good way to get over our inner hurdles is to keep asking ourselves the question of what we are getting out of all this chaos and distraction. The truth is that most people find too much order a bit scary because it can easily feel too empty. However, once we get used to a bit more time and quiet, we will discover that it is actually a blessing. It is only from here that our creative ideas can arise. And it is only from here that we can learn to redefine ourselves and create a life that suits our needs much better than the hectic life we had before.

Action plan for step seven

The most important action that you need to take now is:

If you feel that there are still major obstacles that stand in the way of fulfilling your dream use the help outlined in this chapter or seek the advice of a therapist or self-help group.

Step eight
Receiving the fulfilment of your wish

Ah – now we come finally, finally to the best step of manifesting – receiving the fulfillment of our wish! I would like to tell you that from now on it will be all a bed of roses: we receive our wish as in a gigantic birthday celebration and then we live happily ever after. Unfortunately, it isn't quite that easy for many people. The first question we have to consider is this:

Are you open to receive?

Some people have blocks to receive the fulfillment of their dreams and unless these are addressed they cannot succeed even if they have followed all the other steps of manifesting to the letter. In the work with my clients and myself, I have identified three major obstacles that may keep us from receiving the fulfillment of our dreams.

Trying too hard to be good

Many people who are trying too hard to be loving and compassionate have trouble living life to the full and thus sabotage the fulfillment of their dream. Alongside their spiritual and compassionate ideals, many of these people carry strong ideas about their own unworthiness, which is very sad because they are actually very worthy – if not the worthiest of all.

I have met social workers who were deeply unhappy in their jobs but who wouldn't allow themselves to see clients privately because they were unable to receive even a moderate amount of money for their work. I have seen numerous spiritual seekers who didn't allow themselves a sexual relationship, let alone a family, because they were afraid of failing on their spiritual path if they experienced 'worldly' joys. And I have seen many people ruining their lives through antagonizing anybody who tried to help them because of their deep-seated self-hatred. The 'healing potion' for all these problems is to learn to love ourselves as outlined in the previous chapter.

Trying too hard to be independent

Another attitude that can make it hard for people to open up to receiving the fulfillment of their dreams is too much attachment to their independence. If someone is proud of 'not needing anything or anybody', it can be difficult to open up and humbly receive what they wanted for so long.

In order to be able to receive the fulfillment of our wish, it is important to own our needs and stop treating 'need' or 'needy' as dirty words. There is nothing wrong with having needs. Quite the opposite, accepting our needs will make for much deeper relationships because others want to fulfill our needs - everybody wants to feel needed. It is simply impossible to achieve your desire while **trying to be autonomous and independent all the time** –

nothing can enter your life if you are in this state of mind.

In order to get over too much attachment to independence, I recommend revisiting the chakra exercise at the end of chapter four and focus particularly on positive energy *entering* your chakras.

Ignoring the law of karma

Throughout this book I have explained that we need to give so that we can receive, that we have to make good where we have wronged others and that we have to give up the idea that we can get something for nothing. Basically, all this means that you have to live your life according to the law of karma if you want to be successful with manifesting your dream.

Unfortunately, if you try to negate these teachings you will build up unconscious guilt-feelings, which will sabotage your wish. Sabotaging the fulfillment of your dream can happen in many ways but a very common form of sabotage is fault-finding. Instead of opening up to the fulfillment of your dream, you will find a way of finding fault with it and then rejecting it.

In order to avoid this dynamic, you need to try to establish equal give and take in all your dealings with other people, you need to be willing to give as much as you would like to receive and you need to remove your guilt-feelings, as explained in the previous chapter.

The best way to find out if you are ready to receive

your dream is to revisit the chakra exercise at the end of chapter four and focus primarily on positive energy *entering* your chakras. Carefully look out for even the most shadowy resistance to receive. If you find any blocks rejoice because you now have the chance to remove these obstacles by using one of the exercises in this book. If you practice in this way, it will only be a matter of time until your resistance to receive will dissolve.

Don't make bad compromises

Before we can finally settle down with our magic parcel, we need to be able to distinguish it from all the other parcels that look equally enticing but which are nothing but fakes.

On our path of manifestation we will discover that the universe sometimes 'throws' possible 'wish-fulfillments' at us and that it is *our* task to reject whatever is not in complete alignment with our heart-wish. We will also discover that, as we come nearer and nearer to our aim, 'the offers' of the universe often get better and better so that it will be even more difficult to decide which option to finally settle down with. We may have to decide many times over whether we have finally found our heart-wish or whether we should hang on for a little while longer and wait for something or someone better.

These decisions can sometimes be real agony. As a friend of mine put it who was looking for a soulmate, 'We are presented with a succession of ever more delicious puddings and we can't really tuck into any of them'. She is right, we can't always eat all these puddings. We must make a decision whether we accept a certain job or whether we should rather wait for a better one. We can't do both. Nor can we start a serious relationship with several people at the same time or buy many things simultaneously. In other words, when we finally come near to the fulfillment of our wish there is a vast potential for making the wrong choice and settling for second best.

Many people have a tendency to settle for second best because they feel it would be 'unrealistic', 'greedy' or 'selfish' to wait for something really, really wonderful.

I am sure many of your friends and relatives would advise you to go with the safe and sensible option instead of waiting for your 'unrealistic' dream to come true. Many people find it very difficult to trust that there will be something or someone really wonderful for them. However, my advice is to avoid settling for second best and rather learn to bear an empty stretch in life.

Empty stretches feel scary and unsatisfactory for most people but, in hindsight, they are often the most productive times of our lives. In these phases we are training and developing the muscles of our mind as at no other time by working with all the steps of the manifesting method. We develop a wonderful vision and experience more unconditioned love and happiness than we had ever thought possible. We are clearing our unconscious mind of many outdated and harmful beliefs and attitudes. And we can discover in the depths of our being a wealth of goodness and intuitive wisdom, which would have stayed hidden if everything had been continuously served to us on a silver-tray.

I myself don't like these empty stretches but I do value the increased strength, wisdom and unconditional happiness that usually arise from them when I can see these times as a challenge rather than as a nuisance.

There is a great strength in saying 'no' to all bad compromises and staying true to our wish. If you can say 'no' to everything that would just be a continuation of your old negative pattern, and if you can stay committed to the one outcome of your wish that would truly make you happy, you can expect amazing transformations in your life. You will surprise all your friends by your ongoing 'good luck' that seems to defy all their beliefs and you will be baffled yourself by how much your life can change. Let me put it this way: If you can stay uncompromising and totally committed to your wish you can become the hero or heroine of your self-written fairy-tale.

How do we recognize a bad compromise?

This question is not easy to answer because even if we do find our heart-wish, we will always have to make *some* compromises for the simple reason that total perfection can't be found in the human world. We might find our perfect house, for example, but it might not be the right color. We might find a gorgeous boyfriend but he might live in the 'wrong' town. There are a thousand and one factors to each wish and I personally have not seen a single case where *all* these factors were perfectly matched. And even if they were, this perfect situation wouldn't stay like that for long for the simple reason that everything is changing all the time. So, what we really need to learn is to distinguish a good compromise from a bad one.

Good Compromise	Bad Compromise
The possibility that could be the fulfillment of our wish evokes positive feelings in us that we wished for on our wish-list.	The possibility that could be the fulfillment of our wish looks very good but it doesn't evoke the positive feelings from our wish-list.
We see a few factors that are not perfect but they do not diminish our positive feelings.	We see a few factors that aren't perfect and they make us feel very uncomfortable.
All the non-negotiable points from our wish-list are fully met.	Although this looks like a good opportunity, one or even two of our non-negotiable points from our wish-list are not fully met.

With this opportunity we can contribute to the world in the way we wished for.	With this opportunity we can't put our initial altruistic motivation into practice in the way we wanted.
None of the things we wanted to avoid are present in this opportunity.	We find one or even two of the things that we wanted to avoid in this opportunity but we think that it doesn't matter. (Big risk!!!)

Let me give you a few examples of how to use this chart: If a woman has found a gorgeous looking boyfriend who has every quality she desires but she continues to feel like an ugly duckling when she is with him, she is about to make a bad compromise. But if she has found a boyfriend who looks not as good as she would like but she feels wonderful with him and she is also sexually attracted to him, she is about to make a good compromise. If the potential boyfriend seems great and she feels wonderful with him but he has done something that is on the list of things she wanted to avoid, she has yet again made a bad compromise.

Bearing the initial uncertainty

Many people are fond of the idea that once they find their heart-wish they will have an immediate deep recognition of it and know straightaway and beyond any doubt that they have finally arrived at their aim. I totally agree that those love-at-first-sight feelings are wonderful and desirable. Unfortunately, as nice as these feelings are, they can be highly deceiving.

Making big decisions in life always entails a time of uncertainty. So, even if we have come to the conclusion that we have found our dream house, our dream partner or our dream job, only time will tell if our decision was the right one.

We need to spend a certain amount of time with a new partner, for instance, until we can be really sure that he or she is the right one – and we also have to bear the uncertainty that our potential partner might not be sure of us in the beginning. Or we might be elated once we get our dream job but only after going to work for a few weeks can we be certain that our decision to take the job was the right one.

Human nature does not like uncertainty – we all like it much better if a situation is either black or white. Unfortunately, there is no way to shorten the time of uncertainty. It is part of the manifesting game and we need to learn to deal with this last challenge positively because it is still possible to falter at this last hurdle. In my work with clients, I have sometimes seen that people would rather abandon a new possibility than bear the uncertainty. For example, one of my clients fell in love with a man but he did not call her as often as she liked. This drove her mad because her dream was so tantalizingly near yet so far away. As a result, she got angry with that man for not calling her more often and, of course, that scared him away.

Manifesting demands a lot of patience and inner stability from us. The nearer we are to our aim the more we have to restrain our impatience and greed. Only if we can do this will we be able to harvest the full reward of this process.

Using our head *and* heart to make our choice

No matter how strongly we feel that we have found our dream, it is crucial to take a generous amount of time to check carefully whether this is really true and to feel *and* think whether we have found what we really want.

We can't rely solely on our feelings when checking whether or not our wish has come true.

Even people who work professionally as psychics have told me that they can't rely solely on their clairvoyant abilities when it comes to their own wishes. They all agree that our own intuition tends to get distorted when we are emotionally involved in a strong desire. Our craving can be so strong that it can easily overpower the more subtle feelings of our intuition, which might be warning us that things aren't quite as positive as we want them to be.

What seems to be a wonderful opportunity might just be a repetition of an old pattern that we have wanted to give up for a long time. Nobody wants to repeat detrimental patterns but most of us do nevertheless. We need only to look at all our little negative habits we would like to give up and yet find it so difficult to do so. If we realize how hard it is to change even those small things we might understand the importance of carefully checking if our potential wish-fulfillment may just be a repeat of an old, harmful pattern.

In order to make a life-changing decision we need to employ the intelligence of our heart (intuition) as well as the intelligence of our head (rationality).

In order to access your intuition you need to relax deeply, feel into your heart and then check what you feel about the possible 'wish-fulfillment' that has been offered to you. If you feel an inner 'yes' and a positive feeling you might be on the right track.

In the next step, you need also to use your head and get out your initial wish-list. First of all, you need to make sure that all of your non-negotiable points are *fully* met and that none of the things that you wanted to avoid are present. Only when your heart *and* your head fully agree that you have found your heart-wish can you be sure that you have finally arrived at your aim.

Dealing with your changing relationships

There is one last obstacle that you need to overcome before you can finally indulge in the full happiness of achieving your goal. This last obstacle deals with how your relationships will change once you become much more successful.

Please don't expect that everybody around you will

scream with delight once you have arrived at your wonderful aim. Unfortunately, many people will have mixed emotions when somebody from their midst suddenly becomes so much more successful and so much happier. Along with their joy for you, they may well harbor some jealously and some regret that they themselves are still stuck in their problems. If they can't deal with these negative feelings, they might even break the contact with you. I have seen it all.

Making big wishes come true is like going to another place in the universe and, unfortunately, not everybody around you will want to come along. If you know that in advance it will be less shocking and hurtful if it actually happens.

Some people also struggle with guilt feelings if they become much more successful than their friends and family. They might be painfully torn between their new exciting place in the universe and the cozy and familiar one among their old pals. Unfortunately, we will not be able to relate to our friends in the same way as we did before once our great wish has come true. If we want to stay really close buddies with our friends *they* have to change as well. Unfortunately, they often don't really want to do that.

The best insurance policy against all these possibly painful changes in our relationships is - as usual – to focus on how we want to contribute to the world with our wish. If our old friends and family feel that they are not excluded from our newly-found fulfillment, they will find it much easier to rejoice with us and go on supporting us. If we are firmly rooted in our altruistic motivation, guilt feelings will rarely bother us because we will feel confident that we deserve what we have achieved and we will be able to share our dream freely with all our friends and family.

Finally – enjoying the results

You have worked so hard, you have been so patient and you were able to develop optimism and serenity against all the odds. Congratulations! Now is the time to finally enjoy the fulfillment of your wish.

If your altruistic motivation has been genuine and you are able to benefit others with the fulfillment of your aim, your joy will not wear off. You will not get used to your new-found fulfillment and you will not become quickly dissatisfied. Instead, you will stay deeply fulfilled until the end of your life.

This is what the Buddha, as well as all other spiritual teachers, have tried to bring across to us - that altruistic love is the answer to all our questions, the solution to all our problems and the remedy for all our illnesses. If we can feel this love in our heart and expand it by combining it with all of our present and future wishes, we will stay happy forever.

Action plan for step eight

The most important action that you need to take now is:

Make sure you are open to receive

Know how to distinguish a good compromise from a bad one.

Be ready to bear the initial uncertainty.

How manifesting really works

After all this explanation, you may still wonder how chakra exercises and visualization can affect the outside world in such a strong way. How is it possible to call things into existence with the power of your mind? How can you make things happen where many others have tried and failed?

In order to get the most from the eight steps of manifesting, it is helpful to have a clear understanding of the enormous power of your mind and its ability to 'create reality'.

Reality is like a dream

The best way to understand the mysterious process of manifesting something out of 'nowhere' is to think of a dream. While we are dreaming we usually don't have the slightest doubt that our dream experience is real. We are chased by dream-monsters and we are frightened to death or we meet somebody nice and we are delighted. Only when we wake up do we know that all this wasn't true.

Now imagine that we would become aware that we are dreaming while we are still fast asleep. If we knew that our experiences were a self-created dream, we would not be frightened anymore but would try to change our dream into something positive.

Now imagine that our whole life is created by our unconscious mind, just like a dream. In fact, how would you know that this moment, as you are reading this book, is not a dream? If you think carefully, you will find that there is no way to prove absolutely that you are not dreaming right now.

Our so-called reality is no more real than a dream.

If you find this thought disconcerting think for a moment about the wonderful implications if I was right. If our existence is no more real than a dream then we could change everything that is dull and horrid. In fact, seeing our life as a dream is a very important Tibetan Buddhist practice because it enables us to take responsibility for the negative things in our life without blaming anybody else. After all, we are the creator of all our dreams. And if we are the creator of our dreams, we also have the power to change them.

The primordial ground from which everything arises

Buddhist teachers have explained that everything is, at its deepest level, space. This space is not dead and empty but bright, beautiful and pregnant with possibilities. It is inherently good and has a living and deeply loving quality. Everything we experience – be it pleasant or unpleasant - has arisen from this primordial space. However, the space in itself remains untouched by any negativity. It is by separating from the love and goodness of the primordial space of the universe that people become possessed by negative and selfish impulses.

One way of looking at the primordial space is to see it as unformed and loving potential, which is at the basis of everything that exists. Things arise from this potential and manifest in the 'real' world. When they cease to exist they go back into this space.

Buddhist teachers explain that the pure and loving qualities of the primordial space are at the core of ourselves and that they are our true nature. The primordial ground from which everything arises is our Higher Consciousness – or 'Buddha nature' as it is called in Buddhism - and it can be found in our heart and all the other chakras within the middle of our body. In meditation, it can be experienced directly in form of blissful and deeply loving awareness that we feel within all of the chakras.

According to Buddhist teachings, it is possible to influence the primordial space of the universe with our will power through purifying and positively charging our chakras.

Through this process we can make our deepest wish come true because our chakras project our reality all around us like a 360 degree cinema screen. The purity of our chakras determines how positive our surrounding reality is and the strength of our chakras determines how much we are in control of our reality. In other words, if we can direct *all* our desire energy (strength of our chakras) solely on to loving wishes (purity of our chakras) we will be able to have the proverbial paradise on earth.

As you can see – it is a simple formula in principle. But as every sincere spiritual seeker knows only too well, it is a tall order to really direct *all* your desire energy on to love. It will always stay an ongoing task and for that reason there are so few individuals throughout history who have brought the manifesting process to mastery. Our task is to do our best to emulate these beacons of loving power and not be discouraged by occasional set-backs.

Where does our physical universe come from?

'Okay', you may say, 'I can understand that my beliefs and emotions originate from my chakras and 'color' my surrounding reality. But where do material things come from? Surely, trees, cars and computers have not arisen from my chakras?' Good question.

In Buddhism, this conundrum has been explained like this: material particles and nature have been created by very powerful beings at some point in our distant past. We human beings are simply using these physical particles to build all the material things that surround us. And we have unconsciously 'agreed' on the physical laws that govern our everyday material reality.

But these physical laws are not always as reliable as they should be. It is proven beyond doubt that it is possible to influence our physical health with the power of our minds. It is usually called the placebo effect. Also, a quick peek into the science of quantum physics shows that ordinary physical laws like gravity do not apply when we come to the sub-atomic level. At this level, a particle can exist at several places at the same time, for example. And what is even more interesting in terms of manifesting – these particles can be influenced with the power of our minds.

There have been numerous experiments to show that sub-atomic particles behave differently depending on whether they are observed by someone or not.

Recently, I saw an interesting scientific experiment on the television that proves exactly what Buddhist teachers have said. The scientists had programmed a computer to produce a random pattern of black and white dots on a huge computer screen. There was a large audience looking at this screen and they were asked to visualize a black ball appearing on the screen. To the amazement of everybody, the computer which was programmed to produce just random patterns created a clearly visible black ball in the middle of the big screen. These people had influenced a physical thing like a computer merely with their intention.

I wonder if doing this experiment has changed the belief-systems of the people who participated in it or if they all went home believing as strongly in their physical universe as before. It is actually very difficult to crack our deep-seated assumptions about the physical universe. Even if we hear about people who can do extraordinary things with their bodies - like sticking big pieces of metal through their cheeks, most of us think about it just as a curiosity. And when we hear reports about people who bend spoons, we don't really understand that these people are not outside the order of the universe but actually demonstrate the *real* order of the universe.

For manifesting, all this means that we do not usually create physical things from scratch but that we attract to us the physical things that we desire with the power of our minds.

Influencing the universe with your will power

There are three main ways to influence your chakras and thus your reality. The first is through concentration, the second is love and the third is sound.

Concentration

Concentration works like a magnifying glass that can ignite a fire when we hold it into the sun. When we concentrate on a chakra for long enough while holding a clear image in our mind, this image will eventually manifest in just the way we visualized it. This is the reason why, in martial arts, the focus is always on the navel chakra – the seat of our power and strength. It is this focus, combined with clear visualization, that enables martial art experts to break boards and bricks with their bare hands.

Love

The second way to influence our chakras and our surrounding reality is through love. The primordial ground of the universe in our chakras is identical with love. So, when we penetrate our chakras with love it is relatively easy to remove our faulty attitudes and arrive at a deeper, more blissful level. In the manifesting process described in this book, we use love as the foremost way to create reality because, by working in this way, we will be creating only happiness. It is for that reason that love is much safer to use than concentration alone. But, ideally, love and concentration should be used in conjunction.

Sound

You are probably familiar with the third way to influence the universe through the Bible. It starts, 'In the beginning was the word...' and then God created the world. God uses the power of sound to create reality. Buddhist teachings agree that sound is at the very basis of creation and in this book we have put this insight into practice through the use of a powerful declaration to the universe. What has been lost in some Christian contexts is the knowledge that we are all divine in our very nature - that God and us are not separate - and that we can all create reality.

A simple experiment that demonstrates the power of your mind

Here is a small experiment that demonstrates the power of your mind to create reality.

> ***Experiment:***
>
> **Examine** how you feel right now. If feeling extremely bad is zero and feeling extremely good is ten, where are you at the moment?
>
> **Now try** to recall one of the happiest moments of your life. Remember all the details of this happy time and relish the memory. Do this for at least two
>
> **Stay with** your memory and measure again where you are on the scale. In all likelihood, your well-being has risen at least one or two points.
>
> **Ask yourself**: where has this increased well-being come from?

There are many possible answers to this question. We could say, for example, that our increased well-being comes from our positive memory. But where did these memories come from? From our brain? I doubt that we would find any thoughts if we sawed open our head and examined its contents. Some people may say, 'our good feelings come from the chemicals and electrical impulses in the brain.' But where do these chemicals and impulses come from? From our thoughts? Then we would be in a chicken-and-egg situation.

From a Buddhist point of view, our positive thoughts and feelings have arisen from the primordial space of the universe, which is our highest and innermost consciousness.

What we have just experienced was a short and very simple form of successful manifesting. In our little exercise, we went through all the eight steps of manifesting that have been described in this book.

Let's look at these points a little bit more closely. The first step is to make our wish. (That was the wish to be happier). In a second step we need to focus on our wish. (That happened once you decided to try the experiment). Then we needed some skilful action to make our wish come true, which is the third step – taking action. (That was focusing on a happy memory). Doing this will raise our vibration, which is step four. But manifesting only works if we are able to let go of trying to control the process, which is step five – let go of craving. (I hope that you were distracted enough by this exercise that you didn't control the process too much.) And voila!, a miracle appears – happiness descends on us out of nowhere.

It was really a miracle even though this was just a little exercise. We didn't take our increased happiness out of a drawer in our bedroom where it was safely stored for our miserable days.

Happiness like everything else in the universe appears out of nowhere, out of the primordial, loving space which can give birth to anything.

By doing this exercise you have been skilful enough

to lure it into existence – congratulations!

Why craving is such an obstacle

When we use the manifesting process outlined in this book we definitely will be able to make things happen but that doesn't mean that we are completely in control. Quite the opposite! Manifesting only works from a basis of humility and, ultimately, our desired aim can only come to us as a gift.

If we have a demanding and controlling attitude based on the idea that it is our ego that makes all this happen, we will be astonished how many obstacles we will encounter. Therefore, one of the most important ingredients of manifesting is to have a light-hearted and playful attitude. Making our wishes come true is not a bitterly serious business. On the contrary, it greatly reminds me of the times when I was child and was deeply immersed in imaginary games. If we can pursue our aims with the same kind of creative playfulness, we are halfway there.

If we look at the first four steps of manifesting they are, more or less, common sense. Firstly, we need to know what we want. Secondly, we need to focus on our aim. Thirdly, we need to do something that is conducive to our aim. And fourthly, we need to become more positive. The fifth step is letting go of our craving and for some people this is a little bit more difficult to understand. I myself could not understand it for a long time. The following exercise shows why craving and 'wanting too strongly' is such a major obstacle.

> ***Exercise: Find out why craving is such an obstacle in manifesting*** (t*o be done once)*
>
> **As in** the previous exercise, measure how you are feeling at the moment on the scale from zero to ten. Ten is feeling extremely good and zero is feeling extremely bad.
>
> **Now** focus on the wish to be much happier than you are already. Even if you are happy already you could be much more blissful!
>
> **Now try** really hard to be happier! Try harder and harder! Use all your will power to force more happiness into your mind. Do this for at least two minutes.
>
> **Measure** your well-being again on the scale. In all likelihood, if you have tried really hard you are at least one or two points *down* on the scale.
>
> **Ask yourself** why you feel worse despite the fact that you were trying so hard to be happy.

The answer is probably obvious. When we use our will power in a way that is too controlling, if we crave and want something too much, we will block the process and therefore we will not get what we desire.

The primordial ground in our chakras can only be influenced by a *light and gentle* touch.

On the other hand, if our will power is greedy and controlling it has become too crude and in that way it can't be used for the subtle process of influencing the primordial space of the universe in our chakras.

The process of luring things into existence can be compared with luring a wild bird to eat from your hand. In both processes you need to be determined, patient and gentle at the same time. The moment you grow impatient and try to 'force' the little bird, it will be gone. In the same way the universe will resist when it is approached with irritation and greed. It's just the way it works.

Manifesting is all about learning to use your will power in the right way. If your will power is too weak and you don't really want anything, you can't achieve anything. But if your will power is too controlling and grasping, you can't achieve much either. When your will and your ability to let go come together in the right balance you can achieve a lot!

Can manifesting make us omnipotent?

If you have followed me so far you might come to the conclusion that manifesting can make us into powerful gods who can create their own universes. Unfortunately, this is only halfway true because there is something that interferes with this wonderful idea. This 'something' is other people.

How often did you talk about an event with somebody else only to discover that they perceived the same situation in a completely different way?

How often did you argue with your partner about something that he or she has just said and which they now, only one minute later, vigorously deny? It is common knowledge that judges really dislike cases with many witnesses because they never seem to perceive the same version of a situation.

As a drugs counselor, I worked with people who virtually lived in a kind of hell. I mean really hell. There were women who were continuously subjected to massive violence, who were frequently raped and whose bodies and minds wasted away under the influence of alcohol, tranquillizers and drugs. I really wanted to help them but sometimes there was not much I could do. In these sad cases, the women just chose to stay in their hell. If they had decided otherwise, they would have immediately been provided with a clean hospital bed, with many months of therapy in a wholesome and respecting atmosphere and with a safe and supporting living accommodation. All they would have needed to do was to say 'yes' to the path of recovery. My point is this:

When we work with manifesting we can create our own wonderful universe but we can't change other people because they are creating their own personal universe.

Even if we succeed in creating a wonderful world of love and light we would still be aware that other people live in misery and we couldn't take them into our world as long as they would not change their beliefs accordingly. We can't 'make' them see that they could be much happier. The only thing we can do for others is to invite them to join our world. Therefore, we will always be confronted with the chaos and unhappiness of other people, no matter how good we are with manifesting. It is for this reason that it is so important to always make our wishes with a loving motivation because we then have the highest chance to impact in a positive way on the unhappiness of the people around us.

Getting help from our Higher Consciousness

Manifesting is a personal power that every human being possesses and we can achieve amazing results by using it. We can become so good that we develop supernatural powers of all kinds and create a wonderful world for ourselves and others. As I pointed out in step three, it is important to seek out and humbly receive as much help in this process as possible. The greatest and most powerful help you can expect comes from your Higher Consciousness.

People are at very different levels of realizing the inherent goodness – or divinity - of their deeper being. Enlightenment means becoming fully aware of it. By being devoted to an enlightened being and uniting with them in love, our awareness of our primordial purity increases and we start to experience more frequent moments of intense bliss and love. In these moments, our usual boundaries disappear and give way to something bigger than our usual sense of who we think we are. It is in this state of mind that we are most capable of manifesting our dreams.

It doesn't really matter if we call our Higher Consciousness by the name of God, Divine Angels or Enlightened Buddhas. These divine beings are in essence the same as the primordial space within us and, ultimately, we are one with them. But in contrast to us, a divine being does not separate from the primordial space. They are literally one with the loving and wise qualities of the deepest level of the universe, which they express in everything they do.

If our wishes are based on an altruistic motivation, we will come closer to our Higher Consciousness and our manifesting will go more smoothly.

Our Higher Consciousness can only help those people who ask for their help and who are trying to live their divine truth of love and wisdom. We don't even have to be a religious person to get this help. What counts is that we develop a loving heart and that we trust that there is support for us that goes beyond what we can see with our human eyes.

But it is not enough to just ask for this help. If God or the Buddhas could make our wishes come true they probably would have done so a long time ago. They certainly wouldn't stand by and watch people slaughtering each other while ignoring the prayers of those who ask for peace.

Our Higher Consciousness can't interfere an awful lot in what is happening on this planet because all

beings have free will and, if they use it to make themselves unhappy, there is nothing a divine being can do for them.

But everybody can use their will to unite more deeply with the divine and, as they do so, they can transform their own life and the lives of the people who are open to their help.

If we work in that way, manifesting will be a mutual effort of ourselves and our Higher Consciousness. In many cases, there is an act of grace involved in finally receiving the fulfillment of our wish and therefore we have to approach the process of manifesting with an attitude of humility.

But we equally need confidence in our own abilities because manifesting is much more powerful than simply praying. If praying on its own were enough, every devout person would have everything they wanted in life and we all know that it isn't that simple. Therefore, the more we can strengthen our connection to our Higher Consciousness through prayer and meditation, the more this help will be available to us when we need it.

How does manifesting work, after all?

Wish-practice is 50 per cent magic, 80 per cent our own doing, 85 per cent the help of our Higher Consciousness and 95 per cent patience. Why these numbers don't add up to 100 per cent I don't quite understand because in terms of subjective experience, they make total sense. Maybe it is because manifesting in itself is a mystery. The way things arise from the primordial ground of the universe remains wonderfully inexplicable. Buddhist teachers say that things evolve from this space like beautiful rainbows and that it is heart-stoppingly beautiful to watch this. On the deepest level, the primordial space - the core of our being - never stops to be a wonderful mystery. All we can do is to witness its fantastic qualities and to use these qualities to find love and happiness for ourselves and others.

In order to harness those fantastic powers, all you have to do is to start at the beginning of this book and take one step at a time. The main thing is not to be discouraged and to never give up. And as you patiently put one step in front of the other, you will be well on your way to manifest your most beautiful dreams. I wish you all the success in the world.

About the author

From teenage years onwards Tara has been deeply interested in personal growth and self-development and has dedicated her life to this quest.

Tara holds an M.A. in Education and has post-graduate qualifications in gestalt therapy, body awareness therapy and transpersonal therapy. She is a fully qualified and licensed psychotherapist. Tara has worked as a drugs counsellor, counsellor for adolescents and general psychotherapist since 1988.

Tara has been a dedicated Buddhist practitioner since 1986. In 1997 she received encouragement from her Buddhist teacher Rigdzin Shikpo to teach meditation to others. In 2002 her Buddhist teacher Venerable Garchen Rinpoche also encouraged her to teach. Tara has since taught on-going meditation groups and combines Buddhist wisdom and her experience in counselling when assisting her clients with their personal growth, self development & improvement.

Tara has been featured in numerous publications and has appeared on various radio and television shows in Europe and the United States. She is the author of several self-help books.

Tara (born 1960) lives with her husband and son in the beautiful countryside of England where she also works in her private counseling practice.

You can contact Tara for personal questions or media interviews here:
http://www.taraspringett.com/contact.

Printed in Great Britain
by Amazon